SOCCER TECHNIQUES AND TACTICS

SOCCER TECHNIQUES AND TACTICS

Robin Trimby

ARCO PUBLISHING COMPANY, INC.
New York

Second Printing, 1979

Published by Arco Publishing Company, Inc.
219 Park Avenue South, New York, N.Y. 10003

Printed in Great Britain

Library of Congress Cataloging in Publication Data

Trimby, Robin.
  Soccer, techniques and tactics.

  1. Soccer coaching. I. Title.
GV943.8.T74 1977   796.33'4'077   77-3390
ISBN 0-668-04266-4 (Hardbound Edition)
ISBN 0-668-04272-9 (Paper Edition)

A Hyperion Book
First published in Great Britain in 1977, in
association with Peter Crawley, by Ward Lock
Limited, a Pentos Company

Contents

Foreword by Jimmy Hill   7

Introduction   8

1 Basic skill   10

2 Scoring goals   21

3 Tactics in defence   29

4 Tactics in attack – wing play   48

5 Tactics in attack – beating the packed defence   61

6 Set pieces   77

7 The coach and his team   91

Conclusion   95

Acknowledgments

I should like to thank Peter Morris for his suggestions and advice, Margaret Alston for translating my handwriting into legible type, Peter Crawley for his helpful guidance and to my wife for allowing football to dominate the holidays as well as term time.

The photographs are reproduced by courtesy of The Press Association Ltd, 85 Fleet Street, London EC4.

Jacket photo by Gerry Cranham.

Foreword by Jimmy Hill

I first met Robin Trimby, the author of this most readable book, when I was coaching at Oxford University in the 1950's. As a university player he was an athletic, willowy striker who had the capacity to ghost past opponents and strike the ball very well on goal when the opportunity presented itself.

There is nothing ghostly or willowy however, about his approach to giving forthright advice, which will interest and inform players, coaches and spectators. Robin gives the right emphasis to the acquiring of skill as well as examining many game situations in great detail. He provides defenders with sensible golden rules for crisis situations and attackers with a set of alternatives for almost every opportunity. He provides ideas on set pieces, how to beat offside traps, retreating defences, blanket defences and also on how to get the best out of a group of players within a team. In all, plenty to chew on, much to inspire and only the completely unintelligent will fail to get something useful out of this book.

Jimmy Hill

Introduction

Football is the greatest game in the world and undoubtedly more people read, discuss and watch it than ever before. Yet, as the competitive element grows and the pressures of the World Cup, European Cups and League matches become more influential, there are disturbing signs that an attitude of 'we must not lose' is permeating the game at all levels. It is this negative approach that is threatening to undermine football; it is this over-cautious attitude that is driving spectators to seek their entertainment elsewhere, and it is this defensive disease that has led me to write this book.

I certainly do not pretend to be an expert as a player or as a manager, though I have enjoyed memorable moments and suffered agonies too, as an amateur player and as a schoolboy coach. However, I like to think that I represent the silent majority when I suggest in the following pages that football will only flourish when players, coaches and spectators think positively again. How often have we all seen games – at professional, club and junior level, in which a team scores one goal and then shuts up shop, pulls back its players into a defensive barrier and feels satisfied at winning 1–0? How often do we see coaches and managers selecting a team with only one striker in it, or opting for two or even three 'defensive' midfield players to supplement four at the back? I am not naive enough to suggest that a 4–4–2 or a 1–4–4–1 formation cannot, if used tactically and positively, produce as much exciting and attacking football as 2–3–5 or 4–2–4. It all depends on the positive thinking of the players and the coach. What I hope to show is that negative tactics and defensive thinking are less likely to produce winning teams, and have no hope of providing the excitement and enjoyment that both players and spectators should expect from football at its best.

Sadly, in recent years, it is the English teams that have followed the Italians down the negative path of defensive football. Those of us who are searching for winning soccer tactics combined with attacking policy, have been delighted by the success of Holland in the last World Cup and of teams like Manchester City, Queen's Park Rangers, Ipswich, West Ham and the new Manchester United in recent domestic competitions. Attack is still the best means of defence.

In the chapters that follow, I shall emphasize attacking tactics more than defensive ones, not because the latter are unimportant, but because it is always easier to disrupt rather than to create, and certainly far harder to coach attackers. How many ex-forwards reading this will readily agree that the game is much simpler once you have moved back into the defence! Yet no side can attack confidently until the basic defensive foundation has been laid, so I shall include an important chapter on defence as a springboard for attack, before presenting many aspects of attacking play, but particularly concentrating on positive attitudes and winning tactics.

I shall also look closely at the importance of wing play, the value of practising set-pieces and at the crucial business of scoring goals. In addition I shall discuss the often-neglected subject of the blend of personality in any successful team and consider the lack of imagination and originality in so many over-coached modern sides. Finally, I have included a series of questions and answers in specific situations which, while never pretending to produce perfect solutions, will help players and coaches, as well as thoughtful spectators to understand the game more and thus to enjoy it more fully.

However, we cannot start to consider any tactics and teams cannot hope to search for victory, until they have learned to control the ball. This is the point at which we must start.

1 Basic skill

In order to win at any game you must first have confidence and in football you will never discover that confidence until you have mastered the ball. In this chapter I shall cover the whole spectrum of kicking, heading, trapping, tackling and dribbling — the fundamental skills upon which tactics and success are built. One of the reasons why European teams such as Czechoslovakia, Yugoslavia and Holland have had more success than British sides in recent years, is their insistence on skill first and power second. In these days of well-disciplined defences, it is all the more important to produce players with the skill to take advantage of the narrowest opening; skill in controlling the awkward pass in a split second; skill in manoeuvering with the ball in the meagre space allowed near goal; and skill in using a half-chance and shooting accurately under severe pressure.

Ball control is the top priority and of all the basic skills in football, kicking must always take pride of place. We learn to kick as small boys, but even the best players go on learning how to perfect various types of kick. There are four fundamental principles in kicking:

1 Keep your eye on the ball
2 Ensure that you are balanced
3 Position the non-kicking foot correctly
4 Aim for accuracy rather than power

If we look more closely at the various methods of kicking a football, we shall discover the importance of these four principles.

Kicking with the instep
This is probably the most common way of kicking and is valuable when passing and shooting, whether short, long, low or high.

If you look at figure 1 you will see the crucial stages of a low instep pass. Notice the balanced position in (a), the

Figure 1 a) b)
The low instep pass

balance of arms as well as head. The player has his head and knee over the ball, and this, together with the fact that his left foot is placed close to the ball, will ensure that the pass is kept low. In (b) you will see the vital follow through necessary for a longer pass or shot and notice how the player is still looking at the original position of the ball.

Practice

1 Place one or two balls on the centre spot and line up two opposing teams along either penalty area, each player with a ball at his feet. The aim of each team is to drive the central ball towards their opponent's penalty line by striking it with a low driven pass. Players go on aiming to hit the target balls until time is called. This is very good practice for low driven kicking.

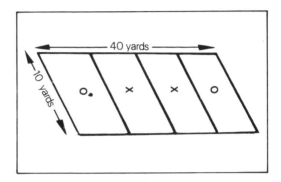

Figure 2 Kicking practice

2 In four grids, forty yards long and ten yards wide, two players try to make long, accurate passes to each other. Two other players try to intercept. No player may move out of his grid. Score three points for each pass controlled within the receiving-grid and one point to the interceptors for each pass they cut out and control within their grids. After six attempts, switch and interchange all players until all have had six attempts at passing and intercepting.

Chipping

If our player wants to loft his pass or his shot by chipping the ball, as a winger frequently has to do, he would *not* place his standing foot so close to the ball and he would allow his body to lean back rather than forward. The outcome is apparent in figure 3. Again, notice the balanced position of the kicker and compare the angle of the body with that of the low kicker. With a lofted kick it will be easier to run diagonally at the ball rather than from directly behind it. As it is vital to impart back spin on the ball, it must be struck below the midline, with a snap-like action from the knee-joint. No follow through is required. The most common fault in chipping technique is the failure to lift the leg high enough on the back swing.

Figure 3
Chipping

Practice
1 *Individually* Practice chipping at the bar from the edge of the penalty area. Aim to strike the bar. Practice in batches of five to see how many hits you can make.

2 *In a coaching grid* Use four grids and play four players against two. A, B, C and D are attackers, X and Y are defenders. A plays the ball to B, X and Y can elect to challenge or cover. B chips the ball to C or D, whoever is free. If X and Y have covered C and D then B can play a short pass back to A. The attackers win when they complete either four short passes or one chip pass to either C or D.

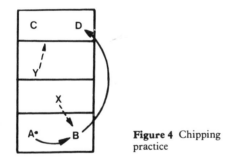

Figure 4 Chipping practice

Bending the ball
Ten years ago very few players bothered to try to 'bend' the ball, but the South Americans and the Continentals soon demonstrated its value and now many of our professionals use the outside and the inside of their stronger foot more often than any part of their weaker one. Bending the ball has certainly brought added

dimensions to the game, at free kicks and corners in particular, but in all facets of play a mastery of this technique can add a lot to attacking tactics.

A ball struck with the *outside* of the right foot to the left of the midline will swerve to the right, as will a ball struck in the same place with the *inside* of the left foot. Reverse the procedure for the ball to swerve to the left.

A full follow through is essential in trying to 'bend' the ball, and it is important to remember that balls hit more slowly will swerve earlier in flight. In fact, the 'slice' and 'hook' in soccer are not so very different from those in golf. In both the striker is cutting across the ball and imparting 'left spin' or 'right spin' as is required. Of course, the unintended slice or hook is rarely as fatal in soccer as in golf, though I have seen some remarkable own goals on the volley from the edge of the penalty box!

Figure 5 Bending the ball

Practice

1 The simplest practice of this difficult skill is probably found in shooting at goal, with a corner flag posted on the penalty spot and another in the centre of the goal. The ball must be swerved around the first flag and into the opposite half of the goal.

2 Four players form a circle, of twenty yards diameter. One corner flag (later three or four) is placed in the centre of the circle and the players facing each other have to swerve the ball round the flags to their partners. One point is awarded for each successfully bent ball.

Trapping

When we watch top professionals controlling a difficult pass they seem to have the ball on some invisible string, so well do they take possession of it with feet, thighs, chest or head. Indeed, in the final reckoning, when we are considering split seconds of time and mere inches of space, the all-important gulf between great footballers and mediocre ones hinges upon instant control. The more quickly we can control the ball, the more chance we have of passing it accurately before being tackled.

The essential point to remember in all forms of stationary trapping is that your body, or whichever part of your body you are using for the trap, must 'give' a little, to cushion the ball just as it is about to make contact. This applies to control with head, foot, chest or thigh.

We all know of the fundamental 'squeeze' trap with the sole, the outside or the inside of the foot, but how often do we practice

Figure 6 Bending the ball with the inside of the foot

13

Figure 7 Trapping
on the volley

this on the move, dragging the ball with us as we move forward?
One of the more common methods of control is on the volley
(figure 7) when the ball should be cushioned with the inside of
the foot, and immediately brought to the ground. If your side
is playing well, passing accurately and moving smoothly, there
should not be too many awkward balls to control. Yet, we all
know how often a difficult chest or waist high pass has to be
controlled and the speed at which it is brought down can often
make all the difference between retaining or losing possession. In
this case chest, head or thigh control might be required (figure 8).
Once again the cushioning effect, eyes on the ball and balance
are all vital and if we are thinking positively then we should
expect players to control the awkward ball and move. *Control
is not an end in itself*, and all practices should be geared to controlling *and moving*.

Practice

1 In threes in the grid. A throws the ball to C who controls
it and moves as B, who has started alongside A, comes in to
challenge, playing the ball to A who is allowed to find a support
position.

2 B and C drive balls alternately from twenty or thirty yards at
player A stationed on the penalty spot. Players X and Y move in to
challenge from outside the penalty box, as soon as the initial pass
has been made. Player A has to control and shoot at speed before
being tackled. This is good practice for B and C passing and X and
Y challenging, but players should change position regularly.

Figure 8 Trapping
on the thigh

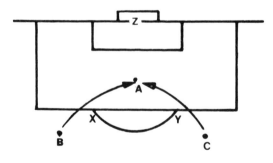

Figure 9 Practice in
ball control

Tackling

More and more we are aware that players are being coached
to hold off the tackle, to jockey and to force players wide. This
does not mean that tackling is a disappearing skill – it remains

a vital one, particularly for defenders and equally for forwards who are often required to come back and mark tightly in and around their own penalty box. How often have we seen the vital penalty given away by a forward, fighting back for the ball in his own penalty area, because he did not really know how to tackle properly? We must never forget that football is a physical game and all the pretty ball control in the world is of little value unless our players are prepared to win the ball. There are various different ways of tackling and this is not the place to analyze them in detail, but four vital principles always bear repetition:

a) The timing of the tackle. It is no good rushing at an opponent from yards away. You must be as close as possible, balanced and, if possible, make your strike when he is off-balance.

Figure 10 Tackle with power and determination

b) Watch the ball and not the opponent. Don't fall for the dummy or the fancy footwork.
c) Ensure that your full weight goes into the tackle itself, and you will be surprised how often a lightweight can dispossess a heavier opponent if he uses his whole weight in this way.
d) Attack the ball determinedly when you decide to tackle. Obviously we must all discourage wild and dangerous tackling, but we are not going to win the ball unless our players tackle with aggression. So when you tackle, do so with the sole intention of winning the ball.

Figure 10 illustrates all these points.

Practice

Tackling practices cannot be fruitfully organized outside a competitive situation and the best way to draw attention to good or bad challenges is during a small-sided practice game when real tackles are essential. But here are two practices which I have found particularly effective and certainly provide the right competitive and physical elements:

15

1 A number of players, each with a ball, stand in a large circle facing anti-clockwise, twenty yards apart. An equal number of opponents stand five yards in front of each ball player. The players in possession move forward, trying to dribble round the opponents in turn, while the latter practise tackling.

2 'Sieve', as the game is called, can be played in small spaces to provide dribbling and tackling practice. In a set of parallel lines, four to six yards apart, tackling areas alternate with neutral areas. The defenders must keep to tackling areas, disposing themselves to prevent penetration of each area. In figure 11 seven attackers(o), each with a ball, are lined up against seven defenders(x), spaced in the three tackling areas. On a signal, each attacker tries to dribble the ball through the tackling zones, scoring a point for each neutral area gained. If the ball is lost to an opponent, it is pushed over the side-line and the attacker retires.

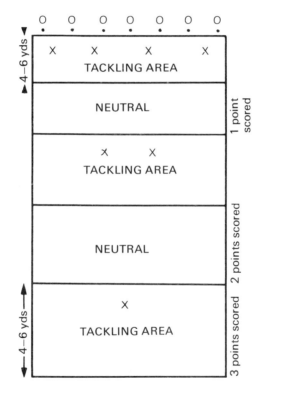

Figure 11 Tackling practice

Heading
I shall be dealing, in chapter 2 with heading to score when it is essential to head downwards, but it is equally important, in

attacking football, as well as defensive play to head the ball upwards. It is all very well talking about attacking football and winning tactics, but before we can attack and score *we must first win the ball*. A team of delicate ball players, as I shall underline later on, might sound attractive, but would never achieve very much because they would not *win* enough balls. How often do we see an attack started because the opposition clearance has been won in the air by the powerful challenge of one of our defensive or midfield players? It is thus essential to learn how to head under challenge and how to time a jump and to impart power into the header. Figures 12 and 13 contrast the techniques of defensive and attacking headers.

Figure 12 Heading in defence

Figure 13 Heading in attack

Practice

1 The best practice remains heading a ball against a wall and trying to keep it up for as many successive headers as possible. Initially a lightweight ball should be used.

2 Using a volleyball court can provide useful, competitive heading practice, particularly if the two teams place defenders at the back of the court so that they head upwards for length and power, and attackers close to the net to head downwards as so often in a game situation.

3 The best challenging practice I have come across involves two teams of six to eight players, playing across the width of the penalty area. Each team scores by heading the ball across the opponents' penalty line. The contest is started in a Rugby line out fashion, with both teams jumping to head. Only when the ball drops to waist height or goes out of play may hands be used, and then the ball must be headed on to a colleague and never thrown. Fierce competition often develops and players will learn to head under challenge. A most helpful practice, especially for defenders.

17

Dribbling

There was a time not many years ago when dribbling seemed a forgotten art. Coaches insisted upon 'two-touch football', gifted young players were advised not to be so selfish and, in any case, the skilful individual was often harshly fouled if he looked like beating his defender too often. A far cry from the original game of soccer when dribbling was thought to be the most important aspect of the game. But players like George Best and, more recently, Johan Cruyff have kept alive the traditions of Meredith and Matthews and it is refreshing to see young players again being encouraged to take players on – and succeeding. It was revealing, too, to note that in the 1974 Cup Final the Dutch side had a success rate of 68 per cent in taking German players on – attempting it 45 times in the game and succeeding with 31 of these – a fine tribute to their confidence in their own ball-playing ability. Nor should we forget that, tactically, the clever dribbler can be a great asset as he will normally attract two or more defenders to cover him thus leaving space for the other forwards to exploit.

Dribbling Balance, control and courage are vital ingredients in dribbling, and this young player shows many (if not all) of these virtues.

But what makes the dribbler and what gives a player the ability to beat an opponent with the ball at his feet? Of course, the Bests and the Cruyffs are born not made, but there are ways we can improve our dribbling, by concentrating on tight close control, by ensuring that we are perfectly balanced as we approach a defender and, above all, by changing pace. The following practices will certainly help improve these skills:

Practice
The lighter the ball the more difficult it will be to control, and frequently the less gifted player should practise dribbling with a slightly under-inflated ball.

1 The centre circle provides an excellent area for basic ball control. Give each player a ball and insist that they all (the more the merrier) stay within the circle, keeping on the move, and avoiding all the other players while retaining control of their ball. On instruction they should use the left foot only to control, then the right, change speed, screen from an imaginary challenge from the left then from the right, change direction, suddenly stop and then go on again. All valuable dribbling practice and particularly so if done with the *head up*.

2 *Dribbling against an opponent.* There are various practices here, but the important factor is to ensure a confined space and to try to introduce a competitive element.

3 *Conditioned game.* Play three against three in a large coaching grid or in the penalty area. Players may score only when they are in their opponent's half, and must always dribble past an opponent before shooting or passing. Understandably the failure rate here will be fairly high, but it does encourage players to take defenders on and if you are not prepared to try you will never succeed!

Screening
This is an essential part of a dribbler's technique, but equally it is vital in so many facets of the game. The Continentals and South Americans still tend to screen the ball more naturally than we do, and I shall never forget my first amateur international for England in Luxemburg when moving in to challenge one of our opponents, I found that he simply stopped the ball dead, ran round it so that he was facing his own goal and thrust his rather large posterior between me and the ball! I was rather taken aback, but he was, of course, only taking the art of screening the ball to extremes. If you watch the top players closely you will notice how naturally they always keep their body between the ball and

their opponents – so much so that a referee often has a difficult time nowadays deciding when obstruction is occurring and when it is not. The photograph below portrays clearly the value of screening, for the defender can hardly make any tackle here without committing a foul, and look how well balanced the forward is too.

Screening – Bruce Rioch keeping calm as he opens the scoring against Newcastle United in an F.A. Cup Tie; but notice how effectively he is screening the ball from the nearest defender and how well balanced he remains under pressure.

Practice

Screening practices can always be incorporated with dribbling ones, but it is a good test for both the screener and the tackler to play one v one in the coaching grid and see how long the player with the ball can resist the challenge from behind.

2 Scoring goals

You do not win without putting the ball in the net! How often have we watched or played in teams which have monopolized the game and yet failed to score. Bad luck, naturally, plays its part but all too often English clubs are so worried about conceding goals that they start with a defensive formation and pull more and more 'forwards' back as the game progresses. We must always remember that 4−4−3 or 4−4−2 can be either exciting attacking formations or negative defensive systems depending on the coach and players.

There are only two ways to play the game, defensively and negatively, relying on close-marking defence, denying space and time to opposing forwards, and then capitalizing on mistakes by the opposition. Trying, in other words to make fewer errors than the other side and drawing 0−0 or winning 1−0. Victory, but not much pleasure for players *or* spectators, and sadly all too prevalent a story in the 1970's. Alternatively the game can be played positively and creatively, and this means inevitably taking risks and accepting the possibilities of winning games 5−4 rather than 1−0. It means encouraging even frail young ball players, insisting on skill first and power second. It means defenders coming forward, rather than forwards going backwards and, above all, it means looking for as many ways as possible of creating goal-scoring chances.

Obviously it is an enormous asset for any side to possess a Greaves or a Law or Müller, players of genius in the box who can turn the half-chance into a goal, but in the final reckoning, it is the side which creates most chances that has most likelihood of scoring goals, and it is relevant, in this respect, to note where goals come from. There are, I suggest, four main areas.

1 *The Bye-line.* Some fourteen years ago a soccer enthusiast in Germany analyzed a season's league matches and came up with the significant statistic that apart from set pieces, corners, free kicks and penalties, 60 per cent of all goals scored stemmed from the bye-line. Athough this percentage may not be quite so high now, it remains true that teams which can 'turn a defence' and get players to the bye-line have much more chance of creating goal-scoring opportunities than those which try to bulldoze through the middle. There are various ways of reaching this danger zone and I shall be looking more closely at these in chapter 4 on wing play. However, the illustration underlines the decisive way in which a defence can be wrong footed by an intelligent 'pull-back' from the bye-line.

An intelligent pull-back from the bye-line – In this case by Kevin Keegan (7) for Stuart Pearson, centre, to score the first of England's 4 goals against Finland in a World Cup qualifying match. Note how the pass is just out of reach of the stretching Finnish goalkeeper.

2 *Set pieces*. Goals come from set pieces and it is a somewhat sad reflection on the 'win-at-all-costs' mentality that so many goals in the English professional game do stem from free kicks and penalties. However, the fact remains that some 40 per cent of all goals scored in top-class soccer come from set plays, and it is quite clear that any club wishing to capitalize on free kicks, corners and throw-ins must work hard on them in practice. There is very little to match the joyful reward of a goal from an oft-rehearsed set piece, and in chapter 6 I shall be looking more closely at various useful ploys.

3 *Possession football*. Scoring chances are often created by the patient build up of possession football. If your team cannot reach the bye-line (probably because the opposition full backs are too good), and you are not scoring goals from set pieces, then you will be forced to play the waiting game, luring defenders out of position, switching the point of attack rapidly and incisively to the most vulnerable part of the opposition's defence – before you strike. It is in this sphere of play that the Brazilians, Yugoslavians and Spaniards, for instance, have usually shown more patience and skill than British teams, though Leeds and Liverpool have proved that possession football can be very effective even in our game of physical challenge, muddy grounds and stern tackling. It is important to realize that possession football does not mean passing the ball square and backwards when a forward pass is available. There are far too many teams from junior to professional who play sideways when it is possible to go forward.

Indeed coaches must not forget that all the possession football in the world is of no value if it is not concluded by the perceptive forward pass, the change of pace, the moment of truth when the angle and weight of the pass must coincide with the decisive run of the striker, so that he meets the ball with that yard or two of space in which to shoot at goal. If you happen to have a Pele or a Rivera in your team then your chances of creating scoring chances in this manner are obviously enhanced, but patience is a far greater footballing quality than is often realized. We have only to look back at Bayern Munich's displays in three successive European Cup Finals in 1974, '75 and '76 when they defeated the leading soccer teams from Spain, England and France, to grasp the importance of the patient approach. In all three matches, for all their skill, Bayern allowed their distinguished opponents to run themselves out physically and mentally before striking for the killer goals.

4 *Centres and crosses.* The final general area of creating scoring opportunities concerns centres or crosses into the opposing goal-mouth. I suspect that if English clubs were analyzed, it would be discovered that this method of attack is more common than any other – this can be the biggest single stifling factor in modern attacking football, if used unimaginatively. How often do we see teams pumping the ball into the centre, with six foot opposing defenders lining up to challenge six foot attackers in a physical heading duel? It has been called the 'bread and butter' of the English game, and it used to prove effective against continental opposition which was vulnerable in the air. The rest of the world have learned to combat this threat, but still we see one team after another, chipping across a succession of hopeful high balls. I recently saw one Third Division match in which twenty-five centres were attempted (to no avail) before either side managed to reach the bye-line; and, inevitably, as soon as a player did so we saw a goal. So simple! So sad!

Yet, while criticizing the number of thoughtless crosses aimed vaguely for some head in the penalty area, I would certainly not suggest that the chipped centre should be entirely eliminated. Rather, that all the other more creative avenues of attack ought to be explored first, unless of course you have a giant of a striker, and the opposing defence has small central defenders and a pint-sized goalkeeper! When used, the centre should be varied in length and strength, sometimes driven to the near-post, at others floated to the far, with central strikers looking for the 'flick on' at times, the direct header at goal at others and making full use of decoy runs across the face of the defence (see chapter 4 on wing play). When used intelligently and selectively in this way, as for example, West Ham have done, then the centered ball is a very real threat to opposing goalkeepers. There is nothing so dull to watch, and so frustrating to play, than the monotonous lob into the opposing penalty area.

So much for the main methods of creating scoring opportunities. Yet none of these tactics and approach plays are of any use, unless players have the confidence to shoot. It is the first sign of a worried side if forwards pass when they have the chance to shoot. If, having made the openings, you aim to score goals then you have got to shoot hard, fast and accurately.

Shooting

Consistent goalscorers are those players who possess the courage, the instinct and the speed to occupy the penalty area as frequently as possible. They also tend to remain calm and calculating in that half-second which they have available when shooting for goal, and all the great marksmen want to score goals as often as they possibly can. This enthusiasm, often not far removed from a selfish greed, is vital in any would-be goalscorer. All these qualities are part of a player's character and cannot be coached. Indeed, it has often been said that great scorers are born not made, and this remains as true of Johan Cruyff as it did of Dixie Dean.

Goal Scoring – One of the great players, Johan Cruyff, scoring for Barcelona against Lazio in a U.E.F.A. Cup match. Look at his poise and balance, and the expression on the face of the Italian defender he has left behind!

However, there are many aspects of shooting that a coach can work at with his strikers, and intelligent use of an individual's talents will soon improve the 'goals-for' column.

Firstly, what should the coach be looking for in his potential goalscorers apart from that physical courage, instinct, coolness and greed for goals? Obviously the ability to shoot with either foot is a great asset, the balance to be able to turn fast, the skill to time a jump and to head downwards, and, again, the confidence, even brashness, to go on shooting regardless of a poor patch. The great Hungarian XI of the 1950's and the Brazilians of the 1960's used to play occasional matches against comparatively weak opposition, in order to try out various attacking tactics, and win by double-figure scores. A waste of time? No, not if used sparingly, for there is nothing like the taste of goals to encourage more goals.

It has always surprised me to see that so little shooting practice by forwards is related to the most likely shooting situation they will encounter. We are told by the statisticians that approximately 50 per cent of opportunities to shoot are from dropping or bouncing balls, whereas something in the region of 90 per cent of shooting practices are with rolling balls. How often do we set up shooting practices with no defenders and no real pressure in sight? For shooting practices to be meaningful they must be related to the game itself, and, to conclude this chapter, here are several ways in which your chances of scoring goals can be improved.

Volleying to score
There is nothing to beat the throwing of a ball (a tennis ball is equally effective) against a wall and volleying the rebound back below a line marked on the wall eight feet, or less, above the ground.

Develop this into a goalmouth situation. Your colleague 03 lobs a ball from the intersection of bye-line and edge of goal area. Player 01 stands near the penalty spot and aims to volley past the goalkeeper. By adding a fielder 02 behind the goal, you can rotate the practice so that all three strikers gain vital volley practice.

Finally introduce a defender (X2) to apply pressure, starting five yards behind the volleyer and moving in to challenge when the ball is served.

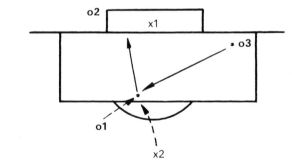

Figure 14 Volleying
practice

Heading to score
The best and simplest practice remains that of using a wall, in

pairs. Draw a line or a small circle, three feet from the floor; one player throws from the side and the object of the other is to head below the line, or into the circle.

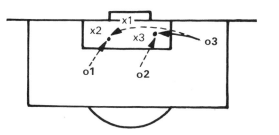

Figure 15 Heading practice

This can be developed into a goalmouth situation with attackers 01 and 02 being served by 03 by head or foot and then introducing defenders X2 and X3.

But remember that in heading and volleying, in order to keep the ball down, it must be struck above the *mid line* as demonstrated so skilfully in the illustration opposite.

Practice

Here are shooting practices which are just the type of relevant shooting situations to sharpen up your goalscorers and keep your goalkeeper on his toes.

1 Against a wall marked with a small goal, six by three feet, try rebound shooting. The first player shoots and as the ball rebounds, his partner must aim to hit the target first time and make the return difficult for the first striker. Basic enough, but invaluable practice to any would-be goalscorer at any level.

2 Mark out a corridor ten or fifteen yards wide, running from ten yards outside the penalty box as far as the penalty spot itself. Station two defenders (you can increase the number later) on the fringe of the corridor and allow them to apply pressure when your forward sets off with the ball. He has to move as close as he can, keep calm under the impending challenge and shoot on target. Have two or three shooters so that the practice flows.

3 Create an area thirty yards wide, twenty-five yards long, for eight players. Make two goals and put a keeper in each. He need not be a specialist keeper. Play two against two in the area with the aim of getting as many strikes at goal as possible in the time allowed. Have two or three balls at each end, ready to be thrown in by the keeper against whom the last shot was aimed. The other

Volleying to score – Dave Thomas, of Queen's Park Rangers, volleys the ball perfectly to score against Wolverhampton Wanderers in a League Division I match. Note how skilfully he keeps the shot down.

two players act as retrievers. This is good practice for shooting under pressure, for two against two, two against one and striker situations. It can be adapted to improve goalkeeping, if you want a specialist in goal. Maximum time in the centre should be two minutes then the players change. When possible goals should be full-size, the portable type are ideal.

4 In figure 16, defenders X3, X4, X5 and attackers 03, 04, 05, 06 are not allowed in the penalty area. Attackers 01 and 02 stay in the penalty area all the time. The free attackers build

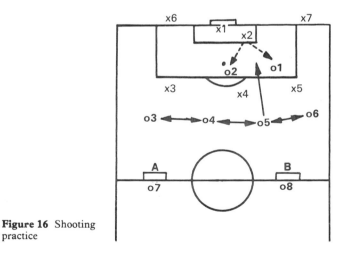

Figure 16 Shooting practice

up controlled, patient interpassing play until an opportunity occurs to deliver a good pass to 01 or 02. As soon as the ball enters

the penalty area, defender X2 can leave the goal area and challenge
whoever receives the forward pass. 01 or 02 must shoot instantly
or lay off a first time pass to the other forward—then he must
shoot instantly.

As the forwards become more and more successful, so another
defender can be put in against them. Defenders X6 and X7 are
retrievers.

Should the goalkeeper X1 or his defender X2, get the ball,
they must try to place long passes through the small target goals
at 'A' and 'B'. For good players, these target goals may be hurdles.
07 and 08 are retrievers who will set up subsequent attacks.

3 Tactics in defence

We have already stressed the importance of attacking football and a positive approach, but even the most exciting team needs a sound base from which to launch attacking movements, and that platform is a well-coached defence. If we consider the last three winners of the World Cup, England, Brazil and West Germany, while enthusing about much of their attacking play and their goals, we will be forced to admit that defences, particularly in the case of England and West Germany, were tightened up *before* the attacking tactics and the goal-scoring confidence were developed.

What then makes an effective defence? Clearly the personalities of individual players should fit into the jigsaw puzzle (see chapter 7) and, of course, a goalkeeper who inspires confidence is vital to any winning side. It is not the flamboyant save that matters, but the authoritative call, the safe handling under pressure and the ability to use the ball constructively. Indeed, no defence will survive for long unless the individual players have confidence in one another, and you can quickly spot the uncertain teams, by the panic clearances, the bickering and the absence of helpful talking to each other, which is particularly important in defence.

Confidence, however, will only grow if the players know exactly what defensive system they are playing. Are they marking 'man for man' as the Germans tend to do, or are they marking 'zonally', picking up attackers who come into a particular zone on the field, a system most British clubs tend to adopt? It is naturally suicidal to fall between the two. I once saw a second division side, who shall be nameless, with two new players in defence marking man for man while the rest of the defence played the zonal system. They lost 8 to 0!

Man for man marking
If your side is playing the 'man for man' marking system, your defenders would be more likely to find themselves drawn out of their normal positions, and your left back, for instance, might well find the player he is marking retreating into his own half or switching over onto the opposite touchline. This could prove embarrassing, but the 'man for man' system does hinge absolutely on the *midfield players and the strikers marking closely as well*, and this is vital if the deep runner is going to be 'picked up' tightly. On the other hand, if you are adopting this method of marking, then you have the advantage of your left back, or any defensive player, suddenly appearing in an unexpected *attacking* position when the opposition loses the ball. In this respect, it is interesting to note that

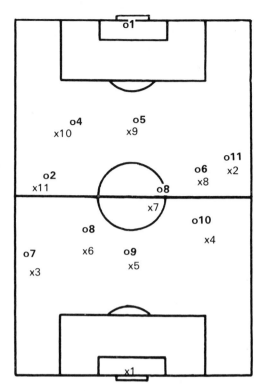

Figure 17 Man-to-man marking

teams adopting 'man-to-man' marking are usually able to attack more flexibly and more unexpectedly.

Zonal marking

This is probably a safer defensive system once organized correctly, and certainly most national and club teams use it in one form or another. The diagram makes it clear that each defender watches a particular zone, but as with all other methods of defending, it is crucial that the midfield and striking players also carry responsibility for marking opponents in their zones.

What an enormous difference it makes to any defence if the centre forward and wingers are chasing and marking when opponents have possession. 'When we attack we all attack, when we lose possession we all defend'. Liverpool have been a shining example in recent years of a side that ensures the success of zonal marking, and let in very few goals, partly due to a well organized defence, but equally through the defensive running of their tireless forwards.

However, the key to zonal defending lies with the ability to

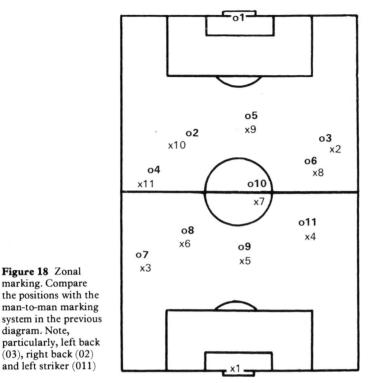

Figure 18 Zonal marking. Compare the positions with the man-to-man marking system in the previous diagram. Note, particularly, left back (03), right back (02) and left striker (011)

'hand over' opposing forwards, as they move out of one zone into another, and in these days of diagonal, lateral and deep runs, by opposing forwards it is, of course, vital to synchronize this 'handing over' and tight marking so that no attacking player remains unattended for even a split second. Talking between defenders is most important in this system. It is always the flexible attacking formations that are the more difficult to pin down.

The sweeper
There are many different variations on these two themes which I have been discussing – not least the *sweeper*. Many teams now unashamedly adopt a very defensive system when playing away from home, and we see this particularly in the European and World Cup qualifying matches where a sweeper is often used, behind a back line of defenders, as a covering player. Obviously this will restrict opposing forwards, though when used in a negative manner this Catennacio system (as it was originally called when introduced in Italy) can be very frustrating for spectators and creative players alike.

Franz Beckenbauer – one of the most perceptive and creative defenders in the game and a great believer in ball practice too.

However the sweeper can be used much more imaginatively as Beckenbauer has demonstrated, and when a perceptive, creative footballer is given this role, then not only can he defend intelligently by reading the developing attacks and snuffing them out, but, because he is unlikely to be marked closely, he can frequently sneak forward and add an extra man in attack. In the same way, a sweeper, doing his job properly and providing cover for his full backs, should give them the chance to attack much more aggressively (I shall elaborate on this in chapters 4 and 5) and enable them to mark more closely.

The sweeper can, however, play in front of the back four and

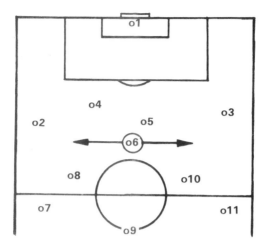

Figure 19 Sweeper in
front of the back four

in many ways he can be used even more flexibly in such a role.
In a sense we are talking here of the job that Nobby Stiles
accomplished for England's winning 1966 World Cup side, that
of a defensive midfield player. Once again such a player can cover
attacking full backs and act as a balancing factor to more creative
midfield players. This defensive midfield role of a 'ball-winner'
became very popular in English football after the 1966 success.

However, like so many tactical ideas which are copied yet only
half understood, the sweeper in front of the centre halves or behind
them, becomes merely a destructive, negative force *unless* he releases
other players (and occasionally himself) as committed attackers.

I have not attempted to cover all defensive systems here, but
the principles remain the same whatever the system. Equally the
players who operate any defensive tactics, must individually know
how to win the ball back which involves an understanding of
marking, applying pressure, denying space and winning tackles.
If your defender possesses these four qualities he is bound to be
an outstanding defensive footballer.

We have already considered the basic techniques involved in
tackling but do your defenders allow opponents to turn with the
ball? Do your defenders mark five yards or two yards from their
man? Do your forwards apply pressure by tackling back after they
are beaten? Do your full backs give the winger an easier angle for
centering the ball by standing three or four yards off? Do your
team, all ten outfield players, ensure that they are goalside of their
opponents when defending, thus denying space? How many times
do your defenders 'sell themselves' in midfield? How often do they

33

lose a tackle near the penalty box? All these are questions that need to be answered if we are to understand defensive strategy.

It is revealing when watching a full match to note carefully why attacks break down. Misplaced passing and blinkered attacking running are sometimes the reason, but so often you will realize that aggressive tackling, tight marking, denial of space, and above all pressure, pressure, pressure in the end brings about the misdirected shot or pass. There is the world of difference between pressurizing opponents and 'getting stuck in', yet both are vital to a team that intends to win the ball and win the match. The Dutch team of recent years, for example, contained players like Rijsbergen and Suurbier who were not only fine constructive footballers, but prepared to get 'stuck in' and win the ball fairly, yet decisively.

There are other crucial factors in well-coached defences and I would stress the following six:

'Backing off' or jockeying

As long as we are goalside of our opponents and pressurizing, denying space, there is no need to tackle until an opposing player with the ball moves into our danger zone (an area extending to just outside the penalty box). Then 'backing off' will no longer do and a tackle must be made decisively. The well-organized team knows exactly when to delay and jockey and when to strike in the tackle; but they work as a unit at all times.

Moving out quickly

Moving out quickly from defence after an opposing attack has broken down is always a sign of a confident and well-drilled defence. The players should move upfield quickly in order to give fuller support to their own forwards and to deny space to any counter attack, in addition to laying an offside trap.

Covering each other

In the best defences, if a man is beaten he will immediately be covered by one of his colleagues while he himself recovers goalside of the opposing forwards. This is why we often see two defenders keeping an eye on a renowned ball-playing forward, and why a defender feels that he can tackle, knowing that he is being covered. It is interesting to reflect that the West Germans were only successful in 40 per cent of their tackles against Holland in the 1974 World Cup Final which, as the Dutch scored only once and that from a penalty, speaks volumes for their defensive cover!

Forcing attackers inside or outside

The best defenders also have to assess the particular skill of their

Defensive cover –
Although Newcastle's
Nattrass has been
beaten here by the
dribbling skill of
Chelsea's Charlie
Cooke, look at the in-
telligent covering
position of Number 7,
Stewart Barrow-
clough, who is well
placed to challenge
for the ball.

Intelligent pressure
– exemplified here by
Don Masson of
Queens Park Rangers
in a League Division I
match against Leeds
United. Masson has
forced Terry Yorath
onto his weaker right
foot, before tackling
firmly and decisively.

individual opponents. For instance, crosses, centres and corners should be kept to a minimum against tall strikers who are strong in the air, by forcing wingers inside rather than out. Likewise, if an opponent is renowned for his left foot, such as Malcolm Macdonald or Terry Yorath then an intelligent defender will naturally force him onto his right foot as often as possible. Let us not forget that if we decide to force an opposing winger down the touchline it immediately reduces his options and we know what his likely alternatives are. Obvious enough, but how often put into practice, even at the top level?

Ball-watching

At schoolboy level, we often see central defenders watching the winger run the ball down the touchline and centre, while the opposing centre forward slips away onto the blindside, finds himself a few yards of space and heads home the cross. Yet in the professional game, even in the World Cup itself, frequently we have seen photographs of a goal being scored from close range with no defender within yards of the happy opportunist. This is poor defence and more often than not due to defenders ball-watching instead of man-watching. If you study a game closely how often do you see a good centre half looking over his shoulder, checking on the whereabouts of his centre forward while play is developing down one of the touchlines? The best defenders are doing this all the time, and well organized teams are always reminding each other of these blindside dangers!

Slack defensive marking – in the 1975 Cup Final as Alan Taylor of West Ham is allowed precious space near goal to put the ball high into the Fulham net.

Centre backs

No side will ever be successful until the heart of the defence is secure, and this normally means the two centre backs building up an understanding with one another, whether one is sweeping and the other tight marking or one playing left side and the other right. They must complement each other and must trust each other if they are to provide the security and confidence which any team needs in the middle of its defence. Ideally, central defenders need to be aggressive, good in the air, mobile on the ground, perceptive enough to read situations as they are about to happen and constructive in their use of the ball, but, not even World Cup teams produce two centre backs with all these qualities. However, understanding between the two, awareness of limitations, but confidence in each other are most important, and if you wish to assess your centre backs, or indeed any of your defenders, watch them carefully and ask yourself these questions:

a) How often do the attackers get behind them?
b) Do they allow the forwards they are marking to turn with the ball?
c) How often does one 'sell himself' in a tackle *without* cover from the other?
d) Do they really attack the ball in the air?
e) Do they play attackers away from the danger area?
f) Do they seem to have plenty of time or are there several 'last ditch' clearances?
g) How often during a game does their concentration lapse?

Answer these with confidence and you obviously have a sound defence.

Finally, let me return to the point at which I started this chapter on defensive tactics – that we build a sound basis from which to attack. For, once the defence has been tightened, not only will the forward players attack more confidently, but the defenders themselves can come forward and be more enterprising.

I have emphasized the importance of winning the ball, but here is the real difference between the winning sides and the struggling ones, when we have the ball do we use it constructively or do we merely whack it upfield with a sigh of relief? Obviously, any team that means business and wishes to entertain will build up its attacks constructively from defence, indeed even from its goalkeeper. It was interesting to note how rarely Stepney kicked the ball when setting the exciting young Manchester United team underway in 1976 and to note how another attacking side, Holland, only gave the ball away nine times in their defensive third of the pitch throughout the whole of the 1974 World Cup Final.

It is also significant that the sides which are making an impact at all levels of soccer are those with the confidence and flexibility to send defenders forward. That magnificent display of attacking football by Czechoslovakia and West Germany in the 1976 European Nations Cup Final, was a striking testimony of flexible attack. We have already referred to the brilliance of Beckenbauer but Breitner and Todd are further examples of outstanding defenders who also possess perceptive attacking qualities, and for those of us who have bemoaned the rather stereotyped nature of English football since 1966, nothing has been more heartening than the emergence at the top of the First Division, of Queens Park Rangers, Aston Villa, and the new Manchester United. All have built up a platform in defence, but are prepared to attack as a team, to play the ball constructively out of defence, to allow defenders to come forward, and they are able therefore to produce the unexpected. All are flexible teams, tightening their defences but putting the accent on positive attack.

Practice

Unquestionably the most realistic practice for a defensive unit of four, five or six players is to meet waves of attacks coming from one another and moving within a clearly defined corridor. Often it is even better practice for the defence to be confronted by an additional attacking player, so that five play four, or six play five.

Questions and Answers

1 The opposition has broken fast from defence and one of their strikers (X7) is taking the ball towards our full back (03). There is no cover at the moment as our centre back (06) has been upfield for an abortive corner kick.

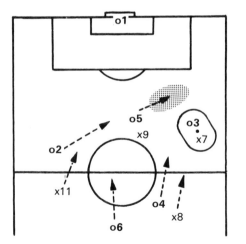

Figure 20 What should 03 do in this situation? Left back 03 is delaying striker X7, while 05 and 02 ensure defensive cover (see Figure 21)

Should 03:
  a) Tackle?
  b) Back off and jockey X7?
  c) Push X7 wide or acrossfield?
  d) How should 05 and 02 react in the situation?

Firstly, any observer would have to admit that team X have done very well to get the ball to their right striker so quickly and to find two other forwards in support, making momentarily at least, three against three in their opponents' half. Equally, if our full back 03 had really been doing his job he would not have allowed X7 to gather the ball and turn to run at him. As I said earlier, he would have been marking his winger tightly, have intercepted the pass and won the ball as X7 moved to receive it – always the easiest and most decisive way for defenders to win the ball – by interception.

However, X7 has gained possession and is attacking our full back so does the latter adopt solution (a) and tackle? Any defender will know that it would be crazy to move in and tackle in this situation, particularly with no cover behind, unless X7 is losing control of the ball. The one way that 03 can re-establish defensive control is by aiming to delay the striker so that recovering defenders and midfield players have time to get back in strength and to reimpose some cover before play reaches the danger zone. We are talking here of two or three seconds, rarely more; the full back's main job is to buy time, not necessarily to tackle. If X7 does lose control of the ball, 03 can obviously tackle hard and fast, and the threat is over. If in doubt he should hold off at two or three yards distance, ready to pounce, but ensuring that he does not 'sell' himself and leave the forward with a clear run at goal.

Option (b) clearly offers a more intelligent alternative. Any defender caught in this situation must realize that tactically he should do all in his power to delay the attacker by jockeying him, just as a perceptive winger knows that he must not fiddle, but strike fast while the defence is still exposed. This does not imply just backing steadily away, but involves threatening to tackle the attacker, forcing him onto his weaker foot and if possible, onto our defender's stronger foot, dummying, swaying or weaving, in an attempt to distract the dribbler. Good defenders are also well aware of the overall tactical situation, prepared to slow their opponent's progress until cover has returned, but prepared also to consider (c) by intentionally pushing the attacker wide or perhaps pushing him across the field. Defensive tactics can differ here.

There are coaches who will encourage their defenders to force opponents out wide towards the touchline, possibly because their full backs are stronger in the tackle on that foot or because they know the opposing wingers are keen to cut inside and shoot, or again because the defence is happy to soak up cross balls. Other defenders may prefer to force attackers across the field, crowding out the dangerous central areas and ensuring that the opposing strikers are not able to build up a threatening attack by reaching the bye-line. This is the advice I would give my defence, though it is vitally important in either case that all our defenders are aware of the tactics. In this diagram, 03 would be asking for trouble if he pushed X7 inside when it was known that the attacker was much faster than the full back himself *and* that he possessed an explosive left foot shot!

It would be very naive to assume that a single defender, in this case 03, could make his decisions without regard to the overall defensive tactical plan, and in our diagram situation we must consider carefully the positional play of 05 and 02 (centre back and full back) in relation to 03's jockeying and delaying tactics. We must rember also that 06 is still recovering fast from his attacking role, and that midfield players such as 04 are funnelling back quickly.

In any defensive situation defenders should be prepared to pivot and cover when the point of danger is exposed, and in figure 20 that dangerous space behind our jockeying full back is clearly shaded.

Should 05 stay with his centre forward X9 or should he move across to cover 03? Split second decisions like this have to be made in the secure knowledge that the remaining defenders are aware of the defensive tactics. Obviously 05 cannot leave X9 completely unmarked, and yet he *must* ensure that his full back 03 is given cover in that potentially dangerous shaded area. In a well-organized defence our right back 02 will already be covering across at speed and, ideally, he should be able to mark X9 as soon as 05 moves back to cover 03. At the same time 06, the recovering centre back, should be looking to take over 02's role, marking X11 and becoming temporarily a right back. Simultaneously 04 and our other midfield players are returning fast to get behind other threatening opponents. Figure 21 shows these new defensive positions and all this moves like clockwork in a well drilled team, much of it depends upon the delaying tactics of 03 in the first place and upon the confidence which good defenders must instil in one another.

Taking the move one step further, if 03 should now risk a

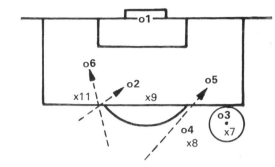

Figure 21 Defensive cover readjusted, as X7 moves towards the penalty box

tackle, knowing that the cover has arrived and find himself beaten, 05 should immediately make contact with the threatening attacker X7, not galloping in to a wild tackle himself, but closing in fast to narrow the passing angle and to pressurize the advancing forward. Meanwhile, what about our beaten full back 03? Rather than attempt to chase his old adversary X7, he should recover *as fast as he can* towards the near-goal post, with the intention of becoming the cover man himself, denying space to attackers in the danger area.

2 Our defender, in this case a centre back 04, is under pressure from X10 and facing his own goal-line with the ball at his feet, half way inside his own penalty area yet fairly wide out.

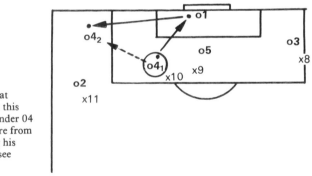

Figure 22 What should 04 do in this situation? Defender 04 is under pressure from X10 and facing his own goal-line (see Figure 23)

Should 04:
a) Turn and play the ball upfield?
b) Pass back to his goalkeeper?
c) Look for a 'give and go' with one of his other defenders?
d) Play safe and give away a corner?

We can take question (a) first and make it quite clear to any defender that it is madness to start turning in the penalty area with the ball against any attacking side worth its salt. 'Play the

41

way you are facing' is as important a cliché for defenders as it is for attackers, and it is asking for trouble to turn in the danger zone when sharp-edged forwards might pounce and have the ball in the back of the net in a flash. In the diagram our centre back 04 is under pressure from behind and thus there should be no question of his attempting to turn. A warning call from his colleagues and in this case particularly his goalkeeper, should remind him of the danger of a challenge from behind, although good defenders are always aware of what is happening behind them as well as in front. *If* there is no pressure at all and his colleagues call 'turn', it makes sense for a defender to try to play the ball forward himself—but these occasions are rare in the danger zone and depend on positive helpful calling by team mates.

If our centre half is under pressure then and cannot turn, should he pass back to his goalkeeper? Certainly this is a possibility and a sound enough option, if the keeper is alert and calling for the ball. Yet, if 04 is to pass back from the angle in our diagram then he must be very aware of the danger which a quick-thinking X9 might cause by anticipating such a pass and running to intercept the ball before the keeper can reach it. How often do we see crucial goals scored as a result of sloppy back passes? More often than not such goals occur because a defender has forgotten to play the safe and simple ball. In our diagram situation, if 04 has his head up and the goalkeeper's call is sound then the *early* back pass is a thoroughly realistic possibility, but defenders should never delay too long after the call in such situations, or the opposing forwards will move in for one of those heartbreaking situations which leaves the goalkeeper sitting dejectedly on the turf gesticulating to his centre back, while the ball is sitting snugly in the net! Further, defenders who intend to pass back to their goalkeeper from any angle, should remember the danger of doing so on a wet, slippery surface, and should work in practice sessions at passing the ball firmly but accurately to one side of the goal, ensuring that if for some reason the keeper does come out too fast or the pass is struck too firmly, it will only roll for a corner and not a goal.

The backpass to the goalkeeper is a sensible tactic then, if the calling is sharp, the keeper confident and the ball played accurately, but it is even more constructive if our centre back 04 then finds himself some space (arrowed in diagram 22) away from X10, and gives his goalkeeper the option of a quick return throw and the chance to turn defence into attack. In addition, of course, the keeper can make good use of the chance to switch play to the other side of the pitch.

In any defensive situation we ought to be looking for the chance to play the ball out of defence constructively once we win it, and in question (c) we obviously find our most positive option. Yet, if our central defender 04 is going to select a 'give and go' pass with one of his defensive colleagues, given the original positions of players in figure 22, then he must rely upon 02 and 05 as well as his goalkeeper to take up intelligent and helpful positions so that he can play the ball safely 'the way he is facing' and then find space for a possible return pass. Defenders should always be very wary of a ball played square across their own penalty area and thus in our diagram situation a pass to 05 (or 03) should only be considered guardedly. But if 02 comes deep towards his own goal-line, receives the ball, draws X11 and slips a pass to 04 who has moved into the space vacated initially by 02 (see figure 23), we will have played our way calmly and intelligently out of trouble *and* set into motion a promising counter attack.

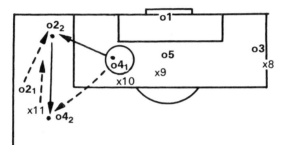

Figure 23 Playing the ball out of defence. 02 has helped 04 set an attack underway

In our diagram situation an inexperienced centre back (04), sensing pressure behind him and facing his own goal-line will inevitably be tempted to play safe and kick the ball into touch for a throw-in or a corner. In some situations it is the right decision. Certainly if X11 follows 02 tightly when he tries to make an angle to assist 04, and if X9 quickly blocks the intended pass back to the goalkeeper, then our centre back has little alternative but to concede a corner. Several factors are important here. If our goalkeeper is not strong in dealing with high crosses and the opposition is winning heading duels against our defence, then we should work hard to avoid corners. In addition, the side that, continually play 'safe' soon plays negatively, and the goalkeeper's confidence declines rapidly if he is looking for the pass back which his defenders are too frightened to give him. Confidence is a vicious circle in football and the more sides discover that they can play the ball constructively out of defence, the more they gain trust in each other. Finally, all defenders ought to remember that if they are kicking the ball out of play, then they should hammer it strongly into touch *not* in order to waste time, but to gain time for their forwards and midfield players to take up marking positions and give a period of calm which affords a much-needed breathing space.

3 Our full back, 02, has come away with the ball from a defensive situation and is confronted with various attacking possibilities.

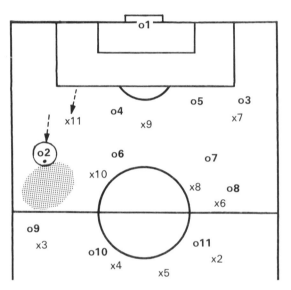

Figure 24 What should full back 02 do in this situation as he comes away with the ball from a defensive position? (see Figures 25 and 26)

Should 02:
a) Carry the ball forward as far as he can before passing?
b) Pass to his centre forward?
c) Feed his winger?
d) Play it square to a midfield colleague?

As always everything hinges upon the position of other players, the type of attacking game that we are playing and the individual skill of our full back (in this case 02). But if we look at our diagram situation, we are immediately aware that 02 has stolen four or five yards on his opponent X11 and has twenty yards or so of shaded space in front of him. Many full backs would be tempted to use this space, moving upfield with the ball at their feet while looking for the telling pass, and indeed option (a) might be correct *if* our centre forward and right winger are at the moment tightly marked and *if* our right back 02 dribbles forward *at speed* in an attempt to commit an opposing defender, hopefully X3, as soon as possible. If in doubt it is always good policy to run at the opposing defenders fast. If they back off, go on running, for this can often lead to a three against three or even four against three situation in favour of our attack. It is poor policy to walk or meander forward in such a situation, thus giving X11 in the diagram a chance to recover and perhaps tackle, and losing any chance of exploiting the gaps in an opposing defence before they are plugged. *Remember that any team is at its most vulnerable when committed to attack,* and if we are prepared to break out fast and accurately and throw support players forward we can set up two against two or three against three situations before the opposing defence reorganizes itself.

So by all means consider option (a), but without doubt the answer to this question must be (b) or (c) if either our centre forward or our right striker is in space and if there is a chance of a quick break. Our full back 02 can always continue in support even if he does give an early pass to one of his strikers. Goal scoring can be simple enough if players are prepared to run for each other and of course if 02 plays a quick driven or chipped pass to 010 who heads it down at an angle behind X3 for 09 to run onto (see figure 25) then our right striker is well on the way to a telling shot at goal. Simple and incisive. Or, indeed, our centre forward might be better on the ground than in the air, in which case the driven low pass to 010 for him to lay it off to 09, 06 or 011, turn, and take a sharp return ball played behind X4, equally suggests that an early pass to the centre forward might well prove 02's best choice.

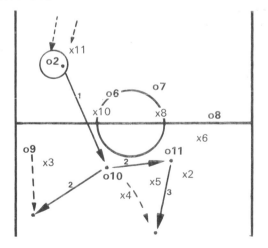

Figure 25 An early pass from full back 02 to centre forward 010 can produce several attacking situations

Alternatively, the full back might play the early ball to our striker 09, who would need to come wide and deep as late as possible, and then pose problems for X3 by running in support inside, or better still outside, 09 and threatening an overlap run, giving his winger the choice of slipping the ball down the line for the overlapping full back or using him as a decoy to fox X3 and cutting inside with the ball himself.

Options (b) and (c) offer attractive possibilities then, but what are the arguments in favour of (d) playing the ball square to a midfield colleague? As I have made clear elsewhere in this book the safety, square possession pass has become the bane of so much modern soccer. Of course, we have to play the ball square occasionally and the thirty yard square ball switching the point of attack is a very vital weapon against the packed defence, but what is the point of passing the ball square when there is an equally good forward pass available? *Every footballer who means business should look for the forward pass first and the square past last.* Frequently we see players passing the ten yard square ball when they themselves have no immediate pressure on them, and all too often the 'square ball' complex indicates lack of confidence in a team, the fear that the ball might be given away if a more decisive forward pass is made. Of course the square pass is normally a safer pass, but the forward ball always searches for higher stakes and if our forwards are running intelligently and if there is any sign of gaps in the opposing defence let us encourage players to look for the pass which does most damage and only resort to the short square pass if all other avenues are closed. Thus in diagram 24, only if our full back 02 is confronted by a marking opponent and he cannot slip the ball forward to

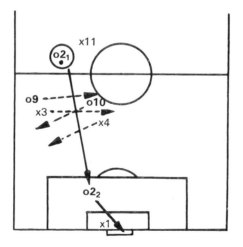

Figure 26 The goal of the season!

his winger 09 or to his centre forward 010 should he think of passing square to 06 (who would need to come *deep away* from X10) or 07 if he were still unmarked.

To conclude, what about this goal for our full back to talk about for the rest of the season (figure 26): 02 runs seventy yards with the ball while 010 and 09 employ two lethal decoy runs, dragging bemused defenders with them. More unlikely goals have been scored!

4 Our side is two to one down with only about five minutes of the match remaining and our goalkeeper has the ball.

Should he:

a) Get rid of the ball as quickly as possible in the general direction of our opponents' goal?

b) Use his area and *then* kick long and high downfield towards a particular player?

c) Throw the ball to the nearest unmarked colleague?

In such situations the immediate reaction of the spectators and often the players, is to encourage (a) and to hope for a defensive mistake or a moment of opportunism by our strikers, a gamble which sometimes is rewarded. Yet, surely (b) has much more chance of success than (a), particularly if our goalkeeper has used his area fully and then steadied himself in order to try to find our tall striker in the air? Much will depend upon whether our central attackers have been winning the aerial duel with opposing defenders during the game, and the relative size and strength of the opposing centre halves. Equally, there is no value in finding our centre forward's head, unless there is a player prepared to run for the 'flick on' or a runner in support. There are two other factors that spectators often fail to assess, the wind, which might make a long kick sensible in one half but not the other, and a substitution, which might alter the tactics of our goalkeeper's distribution entirely.

Indeed, very often (c) is the best option for a goalkeeper, even with a few minutes of a match to play, for at least we should be ensured of possession. The long flat throw to an unmarked midfield player is more positive than a short throw to the assisting full back. It is interesting to note how often players rush at things and forget 'tactics' in the last five minutes of any game. How often have you seen a side panic with a series of high balls into the opposing penalty area, rushed throws and free kicks and risky long passes, when there is still time to keep one's head, and play to a system and score?

4 Tactics in attack – wing play

Sir Alf Ramsey and his 1966 World Cup winning team deserved the praises heaped upon them, but quite unintentionally they provided a dangerous 'red-herring' to English football in the shape of 4–3–3. When operated properly this system is flexible and enables the full backs to overlap, attacking down the touchlines as the old-fashioned wingers used to do. However, 4–3–3 requires a perceptive cover centre half, aggressive attacking full backs, intelligent lateral running by the three strikers and a high degree of fitness within the team as a whole. Indeed, the very reason why Sir Alf turned to 4–3–3 lay in the dearth of good wingers playing in England at the time. Since 1966 we have all seen the 4–3–3 system copied, often misunderstood and frequently turned into a defensive formation of seven, with three strikers who never move within ten yards of the touchlines. I once saw Oxford playing Cambridge at Wembley when both sides were operating a 4–3–3 system and at the end of the match, significantly a 0–0 draw, the grass within ten yards of either touchline was as good as new and that on a wet and slippery afternoon too!

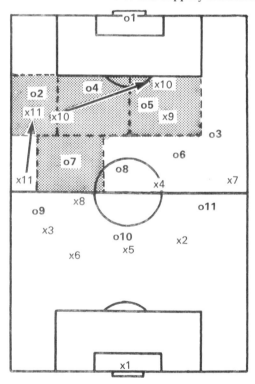

Figure 27 Zonal marking 4–3–3 (team 0) opposed to 4–4–2 (team X). Each defender watches a particular area, for example, right back, 02, guards the shaded square around him and will not follow X10 if he moves across field, but will remain in his zone ready to mark any other attacker, such as X11, who appears there. X10 will be picked up by 04 or 05 depending on which zone he enters.

Do not misunderstand me, 4–3–3 coached intelligently can still be an exciting attacking system, but if your team is playing 4–3–3 ask yourself if the players are operating it imaginatively and whether they are really using the width of the pitch?

Likewise 4–4–2 sounds miserably defensive, and often is, particularly at the start of any game or, under the unambitious coach, when a team is leading one nil and decides to withdraw and protect the two points. Yet, used flexibly, by the adventurous coach, this system can also produce magical, attacking football, though once again the tactical formation should be shaped around the players available and not vice-versa. This elementary fact is crucial to any successful side. Yet how often do we see coaches prepared to change their own pet system to adapt to different players? 4–4–2, for instance, depends fundamentally upon two mobile strong and industrious front runners, who will need to play intelligently with each other, combined with strong support for these front strikers. When played flexibly, as in recent years by the Queen's Park Rangers side, that support might come from any of the midfield four yet it might equally come from one of the back four, and it is these runs from deep in defence that so often catch an opposing defence by surprise. Nonetheless, as with 4–3–3, so with 4–4–2 it is the ability to fill the spaces along either touchline that is crucial. Teams that are well coached will always concentrate on giving this width to their attacking play, whether it is an orthodox winger, an overlapping full back, a central striker moving wide or a midfield player stealing up on the blind side does not matter, as long as someone is stretching the opposing defence.

Coaches can often find the real answers to success by asking defenders and attackers what they like or fear most in opposing players and in the opposition's tactics. It is my experience that defenders, above all, are pleased to play against forwards who run in straight lines up and down the pitch and rarely diagonally or laterally, forwards who always slow the game down or lay the ball off *and forwards who bunch and fail to stretch the defence*.

Many spectators are never aware of the importance of stretching a defence, and watching the game on television or at ground level, as is the case in most stadiums, you have little chance of assessing the width of an attack or tactical systems of any sort. But, if you can gain a bird's eye view of the game, you will soon become aware of the need to stretch a defence by attacking down the touchlines.

Compare figure 28 with figure 29 and you will see how much easier it is for a defender to deny space and to mark tight in the first diagram and the spaces created between and behind defenders in the second. Obviously the touchline player, who does

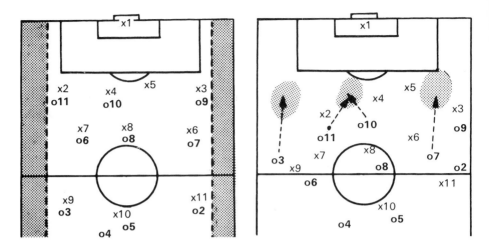

Figure 28 Attackers making it easier for defenders to mark, by bunching and not using the width of the pitch (compare with Figure 29, on the right)

Figure 29 Attackers stretching defenders and creating dangerous spaces for 03, 07, 010, 011 to exploit

not have to be a winger, would hope to reach the goal-line if possible, but even if he does not, look at the potential space which midfield player 07 can now run into compared with his option in figure 28. Look, too, at the greater gaps in the X defence in figure 29 now that they are stretched.

If we want to win then we must fill that space down the wings. One of the more exciting developments in English football over the past few seasons has undoubtedly been the re-emergence of the genuine winger. Many older readers will remember the magic of Stanley Matthews or Tom Finney, and in successive World Cups we recall the match-winning contributions of Gento, Grabowski, Jairhzino and Gadocha. Many English teams have played one winger, switching him from flank to flank, such as James of Derby, Thomas of Q.P.R. and Heighway of Liverpool, yet no one had the courage to reintroduce two wingers at the top level until Tommy Docherty presented his invigorating new Manchester United. Both Hill and Coppell have the confidence

The re-emergence of wing play — underlined here by Steve Coppell of Manchester United as he bursts between Webb and Abbott of Queen's Park Rangers. Skill, speed and confidence personified.

and the skill to run at full backs, take them on and come back for more. We shall have to see whether this marks the return of the genuine winger and 4—2—4, or whether these young United players will burn themselves out or be firmly put in their place, but I rather hope not!

We have looked so far at the importance of stretching a defence and the way in which this can be done, if the coach is doing his job, in a 4—3—3, 4—4—2 or 4—2—4 system, or any variation on these themes, but now that we have got players moving down the touchline what should they be looking for once they receive the ball? I shall be analyzing in more detail the relative merits of the various options open in such a situation in my question and answer section at the end of this chapter, but let us look first at the possibilities facing our winger with the ball at his feet.

Reaching the bye-line

This is a primary aim unless the opposing defence is so naive as to allow your wing man to stride through and score. We have already seen in chapter 2 the statistical value of reaching the bye-line (or goal-line) and there are various ways of getting there:

a) Running onto a long through ball, behind the opposing full back, though no full back (or cover centre half) worth his salt should allow such a pass to succeed.

b) Taking on the full back and going past him on the outside, though again the perceptive cover centre-half should be anticipating this move.

c) Holding the ball until a central striker moves laterally into the touchline space ahead, but a sharp defence might catch him offside unless you are careful here.

d) Dwelling on the ball until an overlapping colleague, probably the full-back, moves through on the outside to receive a short through pass.

e) Playing the ball inside to a support player, a midfield or centre forward perhaps, and running for the return pass. The old 'wall pass' simple enough and still effective if well timed.

Cutting inside the full back

It could be that you have in your team a left-footed player on the right wing, which would be unusual unless he is being used alternately on the right and left touchlines, or that the opposing full back is particularly weak on his 'inside foot', or it might be that you have a central striker who likes to move wide, taking a marking defender with him and thus creating space for your flanker to cut inside. In such circumstances it might trouble the opposing defence if the wing man moves inside with the ball, plays a 'one-two' with the central striker and has a shot at goal.

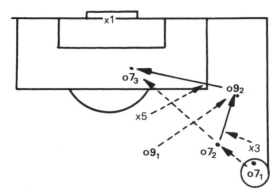

Figure 30 Cutting inside the full back. 07 plays a 'one-two' with 09 and moves onto the return pass

Yet defences, on the whole, prefer to see wingers cutting inside and running across the field rather than reaching the goal-line, so it is always vital to assess what the full back likes least, before being forced inside. How often have you seen forward lines cramped and bunched by a winger who is constantly cutting inside? As in so many situations, variation is the answer and class wingers should be prepared to go inside or outside their full back, always remembering that the bye-line usually provides the greater dividends.

Centering or crossing the ball
The last thing for a winger to attempt is the hopeful centre into the middle of a large opposing defence, but we have all seen teams that score numerous goals from touchline centres and there is no doubt that *intelligent* and *varied* use of the cross can unsettle even the best defence. There are probably three types of cross most likely to trouble defenders and I do not include the high lob which is so much more difficult to head on than the driven or chipped ball and will only prove effective when the opposing goalkeeper is already a bundle of nerves! Crosses should always be played into areas nearest goal which defenders find most difficult to police, namely the near-post and the far-post.

1 *The low-driven cross* This is always more effective if played from as near the bye-line as possible. It should not be confused with the pull-back along the ground (see figure 31), wrong-footing defenders and laid in the path of late-running attackers (note the starting positions of 08 and 04). The success of the low-driven cross depends on two factors. Firstly, the ability of the winger, or the

overlapping full back, to drive the ball low, at head-height or lower. Secondly, the ability of the midfield players or the strikers to make a delayed run across the face of the defence to the near-post, as shown in figure 32.

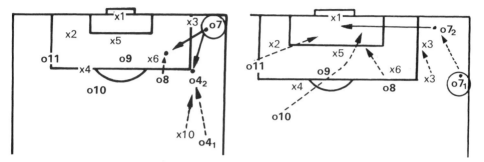

When Peters and Hurst were playing together for West Ham they were masters at the near-post run, often one going early as a decoy and the other coming late and thus unmarked, to glide the ball into the net, either with his head, or by turning it in on the volley. This driven ball has the advantage of catching defenders on the wrong foot with the possibility of an own goal, even if the forwards do not actually make contact themselves.

Figure 31 (left) The pull-back from the bye-line for 04 or 08 to run onto

Figure 32 (right) The low-driven cross for 010 or 011 to meet

2 *The near-post chip* This can again be most damaging to defenders when played from the bye-line, but it can be struck early, as long as it is aimed at the danger area and the striking forwards are looking for the synchronized run. The weighting of such a pass is always important and in such cases the incoming colleague has the option of touching the ball goalwards or flicking the ball across the face of the goal, often with the head, for a supporting attacker to bang home. Liverpool have scored numerous goals in this manner, often with Keegan touching the ball onto Toshack or vice-versa, but the move depends largely on the timing and

Keegan Scores – and his delight is understandable as this goal against Wolverhampton Wanderers clinched the Division I League Title in 1976 for Liverpool; and it came from a Toshack 'flick-on'.

weighting of the near-post cross itself. It needs constant practice and can, of course, be valuable at free kicks and long throws too.

3 *The far-post cross* Ideally this should be used as a variation of the near-post ball and again this sort of chip is more effective when delivered from as wide an angle as possible. It is a difficult ball to hit accurately and is always more effective, as are all crosses, when curling away from the goalkeeper rather than towards him. Above all it needs to be 'hung up' without being lobbed too high, to allow our tall strikers, or late running midfield players, valuable split seconds in which to move round behind the ball and make their attacking headers over the top of retreating defenders. The Tottenham and Arsenal teams that achieved 'the double' of Cup and League both used this ball to great effect; John White for Bobby Smith on the one hand and George Armstrong for Radford or Kennedy on the other. Just as the near-post run is best made by a smaller, quicker forward so the far-post attack should naturally be made by the taller, more powerful aerial players and this is where the unexpected arrival of the centre back can be a match-winning card, as Jack Charlton used to demonstrate for England and for Leeds. Indeed Leeds in their heyday produced all the variations that I have been considering with Lorimer driving the ball low across the goal mouth, Gray or Mackenzie pulling the ball back from the left bye-line, Reaney overlapping, Madeley and Bremner making telling late runs and Clarke always sniffing at the near-post while Jones or Jordan, aided and abetted by Charlton or McQueen, stole round the blindside for the far-post cross.

A typical Leeds goal – as Allan Clarke (left) stabs home the equalizer against Manchester United in a Division I League match, from a well planned bye-line movement.

Yes, variation is vital in crossing the ball and playing to the strengths of your forwards is equally so. It is no good stretching a defence without exploiting the gaps you have created. The following tactical questions and detailed answers will help illustrate the fascinating opportunities that are available on the wing or on the bye-line.

Questions and answers

1 Our right striker 07 has the ball just inside his opponents' half and is confronted by defender X3. He is well supported by colleagues, but the opposition has plenty of men back and plenty of cover on.

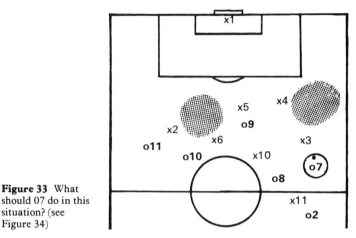

Figure 33 What should 07 do in this situation? (see Figure 34)

Should 07:

a) Take on the full back individually?
b) Give and go with the centre forward?
c) Make use of overlapper 02 (or 08)?
d) Consider another possibility?

Without hesitation we should plump for option (a) *if* we possess the sort of winger who has the ability to dribble past opponents, and particularly if he has already dented the confidence of the opposing full back X3 by beating him earlier in the game. There is obviously no need to use the square pass, wall pass, or long pass if we can get behind defenders by dribbling past them, but this, as we all know, happens all too rarely against the shrewd full back in the modern game, and 07 should also be aware that X4 is well positioned to intercept any ball that is played too far ahead of 07 should he attempt to cut inside the full back. Yet we must not discourage our winger from searching out his full back's defensive limitations and I would always advise any winger to 'take on' an unknown full back on the inside *and* on the outside in the early stages of the match. However, if 07 is thinking of going past X3 then, as so often is the case, he should be searching for some space down the touchline, rather than running into the area that X4 and X5 are already guarding. He can help himself by dummying inside and going outside, but 09 can help by looking for a pass inside and distracting X3 in so doing; while 02 or 08, with a forward run on 07's inside, can again provide the decoy for our winger to dribble past his full back and strike for the bye-line on the outside.

Supposing our winger is not a gifted dribbler, or that the full back X3 has already shown that he can match our striker in skill and speed, how can 07 best make use of his centre forward 09? One of the simplest moves in the book is the use of the centre forward as a wall by the winger, to release 07 behind the full back in space, and run onto 09's return pass. However, because it is 'in the book' defenders should always be alive to it, and coached to anticipate it. Nonetheless if 07 ensures that he draws X3 close before playing the ball to 09 and if 09 comes to meet the ball late, thus reducing the possibility of an interception by the marking X5, and if 07 then moves fast *on the outside* of his defender for the return pass, it is very difficult to stop and even X4 will have his work cut out to intercept effectively in our diagram situation.

Option (b) then has real possibilities, but if we look closely at the position of X4 in our diagram we might decide that the best way to reach and use the shaded space lies with the overlapping potential of 02. He is marked in the diagram, but it is quite amazing (and forwards should take note!) how frequently defenders are allowed to make incisive runs from deep in their own territory, and are only half 'picked-up' or not marked at all by opposing forwards. Perhaps 07 has received the ball from his right sided full back 02, but whether this is so or not, the latter should make his run fast and determinedly on the outside of 07 and close to the touchline. Our winger then has two alternatives, to slip the ball into the path of the overlapping full back, having initially swayed inside, probably taking his opposing full back X3 with him; or secondly (see Figure 34) to play the wall pass at 09, yet leaving 02 in this case to run onto the centre forward's first-time return pass. It sounds easy enough on paper! Nor should 07 forget that if the overlap tactic does break down, it is up to him to get back fast and to mark X11 before the opposition make use of the space vacated by 02. Football, like chess, is a game of move and countermove, full of fascinating alternatives and occasional stale-mates, but fortunately never check-mate.

Before we leave our winger 07 and his options (see figure 33 again), what else might flash through his mind as he confronts full back X3? A sudden, chipped thirty yard ball into the space behind X2 and X5 for 011 to run onto? Perhaps, but this looks far too speculative and will probably present the ball to the opposition unless 011 is especially sharp in looking for this diagonal pass and unless 07 can strike the accurate long ball. No, more likely 09 will consider making a lateral run himself into the space near the touchline, perhaps taking X5 or X4 with him and possibly leaving 07 with the option of cutting inside with the ball or feeding the centre forward in his new touchline position. This is obviously another possibility, but remember that if 09 moves into that space, it then becomes sealed off to 07 himself or to overlapper 02 and I tend to discourage centre forwards from moving too wide in such situations, unless we are playing a 4—4—2 formation.

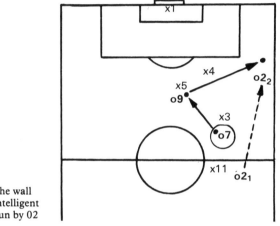

Figure 34 A variation on the wall pass and an intelligent overlapping run by 02

Finally our winger 07 might consider a short pass or even a back pass to 08, and if 09 is too tightly marked, and 02 is not allowed to overlap, then we must retain possession and probe the opposition from midfield rather than give the ball away. Indeed with our right wing build up dragging players of both sides across field a short pass to 08 followed by the sudden long switch ball to 011 might well discover space on the left flank being so denied on the right. The long switch of direction is an excellent tactic if we cannot penetrate on one flank but we shall consider that more fully in a later chapter.

2 Our striker has reached the bye-line, having beaten his full back and although the opposing defence is recovering and readjusting as quickly as possible, there are various possibilities open to 07 as he moves in from the right wing.

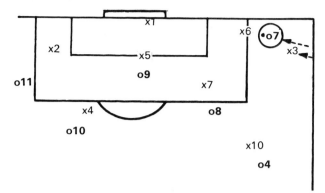

Figure 35 What should 07 do in this situation? (see Figures 36 to 38)

Should 07:

a) Chip to the far-post for 011 or 010 to head?

b) Pull the ball back for 08 or 04 to meet?

c) Take on defender X6 and draw the goalkeeper?

Question (a) hinges upon the positioning of left striker 011 and midfield runner 010 and, equally on the ability of 07 to raise his head and judge his chip to coincide with the incoming forwards. Our most likely chance of success lies with an early pass, before the defence is able to crowd out our strikers, and this will be enhanced if 011 makes a blindside run outside his full back. Having made such a run, striking forwards are all too often tempted to head straight for goal, certainly the correct policy if the angle is right, but the sideways header back into the shaded space in

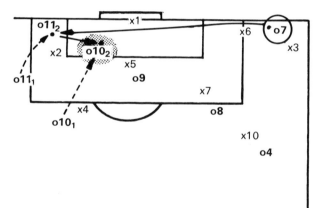

Figure 36 The long cross for 011 to head back for 010 to shoot

figure 36 for the oncoming 010 or even 09 to shoot home, often proves to be the more intelligent move.

Note that striker 011 should stay as wide as possible and come as late as possible, while it is equally crucial that 010 does not crowd out that vital shaded space by arriving, as so many unthinking forwards do, too early. Needless to add, the quality of the chip is bound to be important. How often do we see such lofted passes aimed for the crowded centre of the goal rather than the much more threatening area at the far-post?

So much for option (a), but what are the merits of the pulled-back pass for 08 or 04 to run onto? Firstly it should be remembered that the accurate kicking of such a ball, rolling back towards the incoming forward, is not easy and requires constant practice in order to keep it low. Yet as we have discovered in this chapter, the bye-line striker or overlapper will frequently find that option (b), the low pulled-back pass, is the most dangerous way to exploit this particular situation. If, as inevitably occurs, the defenders are moving steadily back towards their own goal as 07 cuts in along the bye-line, then any forward (perhaps 08) who is astute enough to stop and cut back a yard or so towards his own goal will quickly, though briefly, find himself with space in front of him, as in figure 37. This movement of 08 should occur ideally at the precise moment that our striker 07 is drawing X6 to him, so giving our incoming forward a better shooting angle and hopefully, affording less chance of an interception.

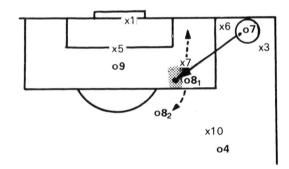

Figure 37 The pull-back from the bye-line. Note how 08 has found space for himself here

However, it might well prove that our bye-line striker 07 cannot synchronize his pass with 08's moment of space, and in such circumstances, it should perhaps be up to 04 to create a yard or two of space for himself, to accept an even sharper pull-back from 07 and then either to shoot or to look again for a variation to the chip. A further possibility and one that I have always liked because of its simplicity and yet its unexpectedness, is the late diagonal run by 010 who looks for a pass driven by striker 07 along the line between X6 and his goal-line, and deflects it past the goalkeeper (see figure 38).

This move requires split second timing and is helped enormously

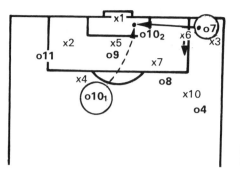

Figure 38 The late diagonal run by 010

by 08 and 04 support players still looking for the pull back as noisily as possible, thus ensuring that X6 is aware of the need to block such a pass, instinctively relaxing his guard on the bye-line pass for which 07 is waiting. Another highly rewarding move! Yes, option (b) has much to recommend it, though we must never forget the danger of a recovery tackle from the once defeated opposing full back X3. He will not be sitting on his backside all this time doing nothing – presumably!

Finally, why not advise 07 to take on cover centre half X6 and beat him just as he has already demolished X3? Why not indeed, if he is lucky enough to possess the ball control of a George Best or a Johan Cruyff, and particularly if the intelligent moving and calling of support players 08 and 04, or any of the other forwards, distracts X6 in such a way as to give our striker the chance to dribble past him and threaten even more dangerously along the bye-line. Obviously from that position not only is 07 in a stronger position to pull back the decisive pass, he can even move in on the goalkeeper himself, dribble round him and score a sensational solo goal. But, if we are being realistic such a solo goal is hardly likely against defenders of any calibre, and although good coaches must not curb the talents of a budding Heighway, a Bowles or a Channon, who want to take opponents on, nor should such players in the position of our striker 07 neglect the more unselfish but frequently more decisive pull-back, or chip, which I analyzed earlier in this situation.

5 Tactics in attack –
beating the packed defence

Having looked closely at the value of wing play and the importance of positive tactics in football, the fact remains, as I stated in my opening chapter, that all too often the best attacking intentions founder on an intelligently coached defence; and there are three particular defensive tactics which frequently frustrate even the most skilful and constructive teams. They are the 'blanket' defence, the retreating defence and the offside trap. I hope to show in this chapter how such stifling tactics can be outwitted by players and coaches who are prepared to practice intelligently and then display both patience and enterprise in the game itself.

Beating the blanket defence
By a blanket defence we mean a side coached to smother opposing attacks by pulling back enough players to fill any likely gaps in defensive areas, and to ensure naturally that all opposing forwards are marked. Inevitably such an approach is bound to be primarily negative and defensive, as reflected in figure 39 and we have all seen the blanket defence stifling creative play in away legs of World and European Cups, not to mention our own League matches.

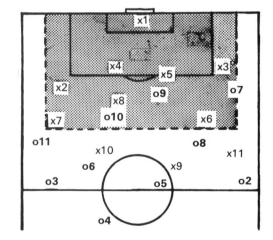

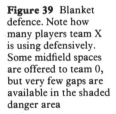

Figure 39 Blanket defence. Note how many players team X is using defensively. Some midfield spaces are offered to team 0, but very few gaps are available in the shaded danger area

While we often have to admire the discipline of such defensive play, the spectacle frequently and predictably suffers. Yet some of the finest contests I have ever watched have been between such well drilled defensive tactics and intelligently coached attacking counter tactics, like a fast flowing game of chess.

The first point to underline is that a blanket defence can only be operated when the opposition has possession of the ball and obviously cannot be organized when the defensively coached team is having to attack. 'Obviously!' you might say. But if we think for a moment, we surely realize that the time when any defence conscious team, such as side X in our diagram, is most vulnerable, is when it is forced to attack, thus leaving unavoidably larger gaps in defence. Certainly these gaps will be filled rapidly once possession has been lost, but there are valuable seconds once our team 0 gains possession, when we can exploit those gaps by a quick break-out. As Arthur Rowe, that wise and perceptive coach of Tottenham and more recently Crystal Palace, always used to remind us when I played for the combined Oxford and Cambridge side, Pegasus, in the 1950's 'the most crucial moment in football is that when one team loses possession and the other gains it. The player who reacts the quickest and changes his role fastest is a real player'. A look at figure 40, showing team X stretched and X7 losing possession to 03, will remind us of the wisdom of these words. We can see the vulnerable spaces (shaded) which no blanket defence in the world, however cautiously coached, can fill for those vital few seconds. *If* we can play the ball accurately and quickly

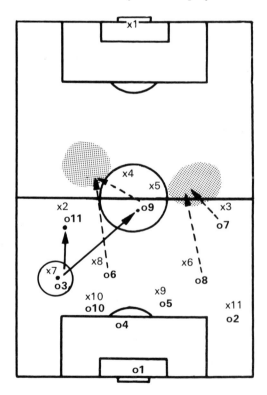

Figure 40 The quick break from defence. 03 having won the ball from X7, sets his forwards going immediately

to striker 09 or 011 *and* throw one of our support players (08 or 06 in the diagram) into the shaded spaces, before the 'blanket' defence is redeployed, then we are in for a strike on goal.

Yet it is worth emphasizing that, if the quick break is going to have any chance of success, our strikers, 09 and 011 in this case, must play right up on their opposing defenders.

However, supposing we do not break fast enough from defence, supposing the blanket is again stretched across our opponent's defensive third of the field, how then do we discover the space and time to create a shooting chance? *Patience* and *intelligence* are the answers. Being intelligent on the football field has little to do with brains in the classroom, but it is painfully clear how much more thought *is* applied by many continental players compared with so many British professional footballers, and it is not just coincidence that most of the more articulate individuals in the Football League either reach the top as footballers or as coaches. Cruyff, Beckenbauer, Pele, Masson, Keegan and Brooking are not simply skilful footballers, but intelligent players too. Well-organized defences will never be outwitted by predictable, over-coached runners, however skilful they may be and however hard they try. As I have suggested in my chapter on wing play, coaches faced with a blanket defence must instruct their attackers to stretch the opponents as much as possible by using the touchlines, in the hope of creating a little more space in the crucial central areas at the heart of the defence. Against a massed defence, which is marking tight and covering carefully, even this might not create the opening we are seeking, particularly if we do not possess the skill or speed to reach the bye-line.

No, the plain fact is that the only other way to beat the packed defence is to produce a moment of individual brilliance or to provide the unexpected. Of course, the thirty-five or forty yard shot can beat any defence and any goalkeeper and is always worth attempting,

Mike Channon — demonstrating his courage and skill in attacking defenders as he takes on 3 Scottish players at Wembley in the 1975 international which England won 5–1.

particularly if we have a player like Lorimer of Leeds or Rioch of Everton who can 'bend' the ball and has the power and accuracy to hit the target from that sort of range. So, indeed can the individual dribble occasionally provide the answer. Attackers like Channon of England, Rensenbrinck of Holland or Masny of Czechoslovakia, are invaluable because they have the courage and the skill to 'attack' defenders in the danger area, and even if they fail to score direct, a penalty is always a possible alternative. Yet these, it must be admitted, are rare moments by players of brilliance, and not all sides possess such individuals. So we return to the perceptive assessment of our intelligent midfield player. In figure 41, confronted by an all-enveloping blanket defence, what can our midfield creator 06 do to open up the opposing defence? Not very much as things stand, unless he attempts the shot or the attacking dribble which we have already considered. It might well be that he has to turn and play the ball back to 04, shift the point of attack and try again to discover a chink in the enemy armour.

However, even against such seemingly tight marking the intelligent 06 will create goal scoring chances if his fellow forwards are running thoughtfully off the ball. It is not possible here to consider all the possibilities, but here are two ways to crack the X defence, and indeed, if timed properly, to expose any defence.

Firstly, supposing 011 and 07 make lateral runs across the defence, as if switching wings, and if at the same time our centre forward 09 comes a few yards away from goal, probably bringing the close marking X5 with him. For a fleeting second or two the shaded space just inside the penalty box will probably become available and if 011, instead of completing his cross-field run, cuts towards goal (as in figure 41) 06 will find that a little curved

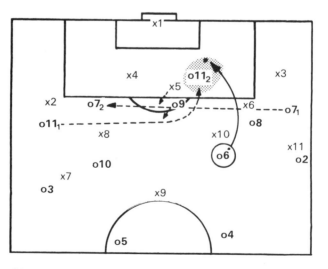

Figure 41 Beating the blanket defence by the imaginative play of 06 and 011

ball in to the path of 011 as he changes direction could provide a real shooting chance. Clearly it all looks easier on paper, obviously 011 and 06 will need a close understanding as the need to synchronize the timing of the run with the pass is vital, and naturally we would not consider the move if our 011 did not possess a good right foot, *but* such a tactic can open up the tightest defence and how? *Patience*, 06 must wait for the right moment, and *Intelligence* by several forwards not just one!

Secondly, the unexpected. Supposing 06 takes the ball across field in our diagram situation towards the left touchline, criss-crossing 010 as he goes. As he does so, 09 moves left dragging the close marking X5 with him, at the same time 07 remains as wide as possible, 08 pulls back thus keeping X6 occupied, while 04 starts to run from deep, aiming to reach the right edge of the opposing penalty box just as the shaded space becomes exposed. At this stage 06, whom everyone is now expecting to 'play the way you are facing' and slip a safety pass to 011 or 03, instead delivers a reverse pass with his left foot, chipped or driven, into the vacated space in figure 42, giving 04 a real shooting chance.

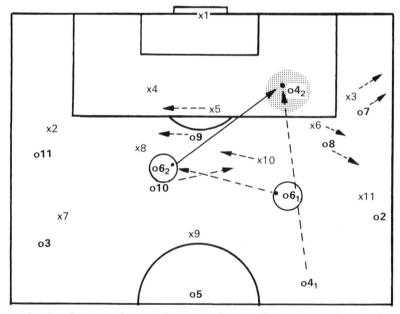

Figure 42 Beating the blanket defence by the imaginative play of 06 and 04

Again the pass has to be a good one, the moment has to be synchronized, but even if it fails two or three times, is it not just the sort of unexpected move which is always likely to catch even the most claustrophobic 'blanket defence' off guard? Indeed, how often do we see this sort of brave, imaginative reverse pass used in English

65

football these days? Sadly all too rarely. Overcoached and stereo-typed English teams, although giving us a lot of excitement in the muddy passions of League football, are frequently exposed by the originality, imagination and pure skill of European and South American sides. Those of us at Wembley early in 1977 to see Holland give England a lesson in intelligent, flexible football, were sharply reminded of this difference in attitudes. The Englishmen that evening ran hard, tackled fiercely and pumped predictable balls into the penalty box, while the Dutchmen relied upon skill, slowed the game down and showed us that any defence can be unlocked by imagination, patience and intelligence working in harmony.

Beating the retreating defence

Finally, while analyzing ways to counter the well organized defence, we should note the difference between the heavily populated 'blanket' tactic and the 'retreating' defence. The latter may not indicate a negative approach, but simply reflect a well coached side which has been instructed not to commit themselves to the 50—50 tackle in midfield, but to 'back off', delay, jockey and buy time until their more attacking colleagues have a chance to recover and get 'goalside' of opponents. I shall be dealing in more detail with the way to trouble a retreating defence in the question and answer section at the end of this chapter. However, what tactics should be adopted if we are playing against a side which is happy to concede us the middle of the field, while they plug the gaps in the more dangerous defensive areas?

The answers here have been partially covered in our consideration of the 'blanket defence', that is the quick break from our own defence, the use of the touchlines, the attack on the bye-line

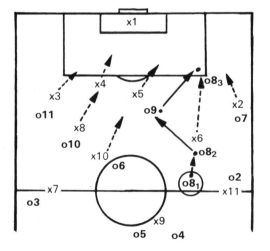

Figure 43 The quick strike against the retreating defence. Note how quickly o8 has to react

and the intelligent use of the unexpected. But there are three vital questions that must always be answered when confronted with the retreating defence. Why are they retreating? In order to slow our attack and re-group. What easy passes are they offering us? The square ball or back pass. What are they going to fear most? The side that runs at them and commits them to the tackle that they are seeking to avoid or the side that attacks their defensive third of the field before it can be sealed off.

Thus in figure 43 our midfield player 08 with the ball must resist the temptation to play the easy and obvious square pass to 06 or 02, and instead should drive forward, committing the nearest defender (in this case X6) and looking to play a 'give and go' with his centre forward or with one of his strikers before the opposing defence has its cover properly organized.

Beating the offside trap

The offside trap is a curse to forwards, linesmen and spectators alike and I have often felt that this is one of the very few laws of the game that should be altered. However, it is easier said than done, and one must also admit that the 'offside game' played well can be a most effective way of curbing many a talented forward line.

I would never think of using the system with a defence of mine, for so much in the end relies upon the astute eye of the referee and his linesmen, quite apart from the damper it is bound to place on a fast flowing, attacking game of football. This is not to say that I would expect my defence to keep opposing players onside! My well drilled defence should move fast upfield, as a unit, as soon as the ball has been cleared, and it serves any idling opposing forward right if he is then caught offside when the ball is quickly played back into the penalty area. No, this is a very different matter from the offside trap.

How do we overcome this frustrating defensive ruse? Once again quick thinking and discipline are vital ingredients. Firstly, it is absolutely crucial for our strikers, who have perhaps moved close on goal in order to challenge the keeper or to search out a half-chance of scoring, to move back onside as fast as the defenders move out of their own penalty area. Nothing is more irritating than the slow-witted individual who is continually being caught off-side. Secondly, we might look to one of our defending players, usually the full back 02 as in figure 44, to start making a run from deep where he will not normally be marked very tightly. Thirdly, our player on the ball, in this case 010, should be looking to chip the ball over the advancing wall of defenders and retreating

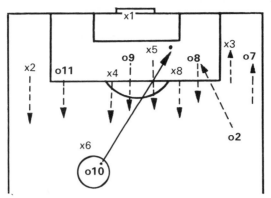

Figure 44 Beating the offside trap. As defenders and attackers pour out, so 02 moves onto 010's through pass

attackers, for 02 to run onto. This is the most obvious way to defeat the offside trap, but it does depend upon the timing of the chip in relation to the full back's run, and as I have emphasized, the quick reaction of our forwards in keeping onside.

The other way to defeat the offside trap, apart from waiting for the almost inevitable moment when one of the opposing defenders fails to move up in line and thus leaves one of our forwards onside and no cover in sight, is the simple solution of keeping possession and dribbling straight through. Any defender advancing rapidly, in order to leave our strikers offside, is never going to find it easy to tackle a determined attacker moving fast in the opposite direction, and the intelligent strike just as the opposing defence is coming out often provides a solution to the offside game. This depends on our strikers, 07, 08, 09 and 011 in the diagram, reacting quickly and not spoiling the tactic by getting caught offside.

There are two final comments on the offside trap. I am sometimes amazed that even experienced players do not know the exact offside rules and naturally it is vital that all footballers learn them. Equally, it is all too easy making offside decisions from high in the stands and even simpler to sit back in our arm chairs and watch some smug television commentator reminding us that it was an 'offside goal' or 'never a penalty'. It is a very different matter having to make a snap decision on the field itself. It would be far more helpful if commentators were to make constructive comments about the game.

Questions and answers
1 The ball is in midfield with our advancing player 04. The central striker 09 has various options open to him. I wonder whether you have ever watched such a player without the ball, searching for the ideal position, trying to find space and to receive a telling pass?

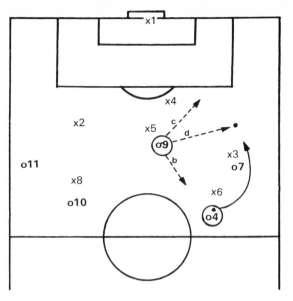

Figure 45 04 has the ball, where should 09 go?

Should 09:

a) Stay where he is?

b) Move towards the player with the ball?

c) Make a through run in the direction of the opposing goal?

d) Run laterally towards the touchline?

Once again much hinges upon the system in which the players have been coached, but the last thing a central striker should be doing in such a situation is to remain static. One of the vital factors that we do *not* witness on 'Match of the Day' is the tireless and intelligent running of the outstanding strikers 'off the ball'. It has been assessed that most players actually touch the ball in the region of fifty times a match and rarely keep possession for more than one minute out of ninety, so that it becomes apparent how crucial it is to be able to play without the ball.

Moving towards the player with the ball as in (b) is frequently far more effective than running away, but a striker must be wary of cluttering up an already crowded midfield and it would be more help to 04 if our central striker in the diagram took his marking centre half X5 away, before 'checking out' that is moving a yard or two back towards his own goal and with his back to his opponents' goal, laying the ball off to a supporting midfield colleague. But a central striker does not need to come too far back, unless a midfield player immediately takes his place.

What about the through run in option (c)? Surely this is the direct type of thrust coaches and spectators hope to see? In one sense it is, but football is a game of angles, and whereas a ball in our diagram from 04 might be acceptable to our striker running through, a pass from behind has never much chance of success, and again should be easy enough for cover centre back X4 to swallow up.

No, the best run open to our centre forward is probably (d), a lateral run across the face of the centre halves and behind the left back. The lofted pass, over our right striker into space, is just the sort of positive thrust for which he is looking and our centre forward's run would be made all the more effective if right striker 07 then moves in support and either our left striker 011 or one of the other midfield players, takes up the position vacated at centre forward. Finally, of course, if our wandering striker is closely followed by his marking centre half, then 04 has an alternative pass into the space now opened up in the centre of the opposing defence. Decoy runs are often vitally effective and the best strikers are continually aware of this.

2 A typical midfield situation, with our midfield player 06 ball at feet, being pressured from behind but with space in front. Yet the three strikers are tightly marked.

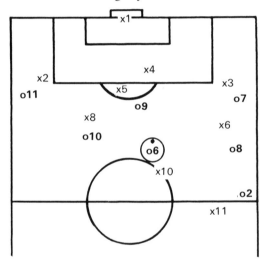

Figure 46 What should 06 do in this situation? (see Figure 47)

Should 06:
a) Pass to the feet of one of his front three strikers?
b) Play a 'through ball' over the opposing defence for one of his strikers to sprint onto?
c) Carry the ball to the opposing defence?
d) Spread the ball wide and square to an overlapping full back?

Obviously much depends upon the style of attacking play adopted and it might be that (a) is the right pass if the striker is 'coming off' his defender and is prepared to play the ball back to a supporting midfield colleague. However, if the defender is really marking closely and we have a particularly fast winger then (b) should be considered. It is certainly the most direct thrust at goal and yet the timing of the winger's run and the timing of the pass need to be perfectly synchronized — and note that defender X4 is in a good position to cover such a ball.

Option (d) should always be available in a well organized team, but *any square ball should only be considered if the more positive alternatives are already blocked,* and though we will now be stretching the opposing defence and posing problems to X3, we have not got behind them.

I suspect that (c) will more often than not provide the best answer against a well organized defence, as long as our player with the ball runs *fast* at the central defenders and is prepared to part with the ball as soon as he has committed one of them. The tactical situation might then look something like this, as long as our strikers have moved intelligently 'off the ball' and have not bunched or run offside.

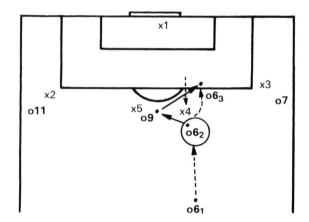

Figure 47
Committing the
defence

The position of our central striker 09 is crucial, but the intelligent player will make a good angle for 06 so that the latter can play the ball at 09 (the wall pass) continue running, and collect the return in a fine position to score. Note how much more helpful 07 and 011 are when stretching the opposing full backs by moving wide.

3 We have possession on the left side of the field just inside our opponents' half and perhaps because our 'build up' has been slow, a number of support players and therefore their opposite numbers who are marking tight, have been pulled across towards the left touchline. What options has our left striker 011, at his disposal?

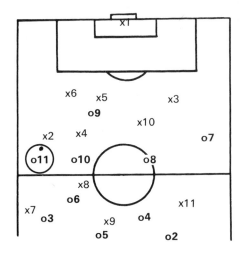

Figure 48 What should 011 do in this situation (see Figures 49 to 53)

Should 011:

a) Try to attack further down the left touchline?

b) Try to open up the play by using his centre forward 09?

c) Switch the ball as rapidly as possible to right striker 07?

d) Accept that attacking channels are blocked and thus play the ball back to support colleagues 03 or 06?

Have you ever watched a football match televised from a bird's-eye view, immediately above the pitch? I have, in the USA when I was teaching and coaching there in 1966, and although the game itself was nothing particularly glamorous, the film, taken from a helicopter, was fascinating because it made abundantly clear that certain areas of the pitch become very over-crowded while others remain under-populated in any given situation. We are sometimes aware of this view of the game when we are lucky enough to watch from high up in the stands, but those who faithfully follow their teams from the terraces and frequently the players and coaches too, are often singularly unaware of the vacant and therefore potentially dangerous spaces at any specific moment.

In figure 48 we find a common enough situation, in which the left side of the field is becoming filled with players, leaving the right side relatively and increasingly open. Our opponents X have been given time to mark and cover carefully and our support players 03, 06, 09 and 010 have to make themselves a few yards of space in order to assist 011. Obviously, if 010 or 09, in particular, are prepared to call for the ball, and move intelligently, 011 might have more chance of using them as a decoy while he attacks X2 and tries to dribble down the left touchline. Yet, if you look closely at the diagram, X6 has already taken up a shrewd covering

72

position to anticipate such a move and thus option (a) is unlikely to succeed in this situation.

Option (b) clearly has no chance of success unless 09 is the type of centre forward who can play with his back to the opposing goal and screen or lay-off under pressure. However, if 011 and 09 have a good understanding, the 'give and go' ball might be worth considering. It may be played early so that 09 can return it towards the left touchline for 011 to run onto, (as in figure 49) or 09 himself can move wide to the line (as in figure 50) thus giving 011 the chance of cutting inside his full back and running at the central defence before releasing the ball.

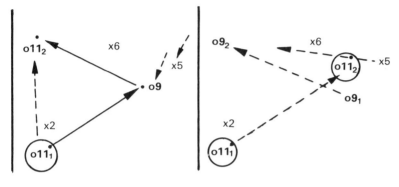

Figure 49 (left) The 'give and go' pass. 09 sets 011 free down the left touchline.

Figure 50 (right) The decoy. A helpful run by 09, leaving space for 011 to exploit

Then, of course, 011 might consider the potentially dangerous diagonal ball to 08, played into space behind X10 and possibly flicked on, or, even better, dummied by our centre forward 09 (see figure 51).

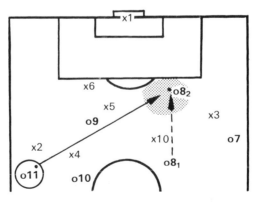

Figure 51 The long diagonal ball for 08 to move onto in the shaded space

As so often in football, we begin to realize the enormous range of possible passes in any given situation, but, although these three suggested moves might disturb the opposing defence, they are all likely to be rather ambitious against the well-organized cover shown in figure 48. X6, as we have seen, should be able to cover any thrust down the left touchline and X3 is in the correct position to snuff out any threat from our midfield runner 08.

So what has option (c) to offer? Well, we return to the simple but vital factor in football that *when play is on one side of the field the most tempting spaces are to be discovered on the opposite flank and the quicker a side makes use of them the greater the threat to the opposing defence.* In our diagram, for instance it is clear enough how much space 07 is enjoying compared with 011, and how little immediate cover is to be found behind full back X3 compared with X2. Yet, we all realize how quickly those spaces will be filled by covering defenders if the ball is not transferred even more quickly from left to right. How do we exploit these promising spaces (shaded in figure 52) which a switch of play would bring us?

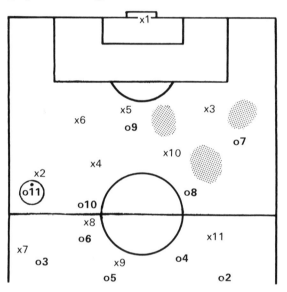

Figure 52 Switching play. When play is on one side of the field, look at the shaded spaces on the other

Firstly, it is obvious enough that if 011 can pass the ball accurately and powerfully fifty yards or so immediately across field to his right striker 07 then that is the most direct route, giving opposing defenders little time to readjust their cover and temporarily offering 07 the chance of a one to one confrontation. However, even Bobby Charlton, that master of the cross-field ball would have found it difficult to strike a pass of such quality and for most players such a ball is too much of a gamble, and might all too easily offer X10 or X3 the chance of intercepting and attacking the equally empty spaces in our right-side defence!

No, the real clue to a telling change of direction usually lies with our support players 06, 08 and 010, or perhaps 03 and 09. If 06 or 010 are prepared to check while the general movement of play is steadily towards our opponents' goal and take a pace or two backwards towards our goal (see figure 53), they will almost always discover that they win themselves momentarily a yard or two of space. This can be utilized by a quick pass from 011, a turn with the ball and possibly a dummy by 010 or 06. It opens up the immediate prospect of a long crossfield ball, though now a more acceptable thirty to forty yards and not fifty, to 07's feet. If driven low, or curled with the inside or outside of the foot rather than chipped too high, the pass will still reach our right striker before those crucial spaces behind full back X3 can be sealed off.

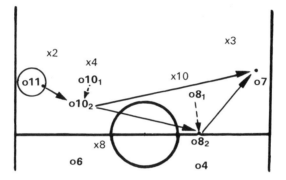

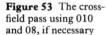

Figure 53 The cross-field pass using 010 and 08, if necessary

Such a decisive switch of play can also be made via 09 or 03, or by the direct cross-field pass to 08, but in these cases there are usually greater risks and less chance of an accurate pass. However, if 010 in the diagram situation cannot for any reason find 07 directly then he might well have to pass the ball to 08 or 04 en route to the right touchline. In this case our switch of direction has again been achieved, but remember how many more vital seconds the opposing defence now gains in swivelling and readjusting its cover.

Rather than give the ball away by looking for the over-ambitious pass, it is usually better to retain possession and start to build up an attack all over again. Thus, in this situation in figure 52, if all other attacking avenues are blocked and we cannot go forwards, nor can 011 see the chance of the sudden switch across field, then option (d) must always be available and used. Full back 03, or the centre back 05, should be searching for a support position in case our left striker needs to use them, and then, perhaps by transferring the ball across the back four to 02, or by dribbling at the opposition and committing players, we should start to construct another attack, probing in another area of the field.

There is never a single answer to any of football's tactics and this is one of the factors that makes it such an enthralling and creative game; recently two teams emphasized this point most clearly. On the first Saturday in May, I saw the exciting young Manchester United side defeated by a well coached and underrated Southampton team in the F.A. Cup Final, and, you may remember that they lost to a fine goal by Stokes. Yet it was McCalliog, ironically a Manchester United reject, who made the goal with one of several perceptive, but risky through balls which he gave during the game. It was said that he attempted six or seven of these bold, penetrating passes in the whole ninety minutes, five went to the opposition, one should have been a goal and one led to the crucial difference between victory and defeat. On the other hand, three days later I was lucky enough to be present, in one of those marvellous atmospheres, which I suspect only the English League can really produce, when Liverpool were attempting to win the first division championship at Wolverhampton, who themselves needed to win the game to prevent relegation. Again, you might recall that Wolves were 1–0 ahead for most of the game and yet, to their eternal credit, Liverpool went on *patiently* building up attack after attack, rarely panicking, prepared to start building again if all attacking avenues were blocked, insisting upon possession football and never prepared to take a chance with the sort of pass which had won the Cup Final for Southampton only a few days previously. Their patience was rewarded with three magnificent goals in the final fourteen minutes and the League title was theirs.

Two vital matches won with very different tactics, yet both effective, both requiring great skill and team discipline and who is to say whether Southampton's penetration or Liverpool's possession reflected the better system? Yet Liverpool's outstanding achievements in 1977 seem to indicate that their traditional system is the more consistent.

6 Set pieces

Successful teams spend more time practising set pieces, free kicks, corners, throw-ins, defensive walls, etc. than anything else and, when you consider the number of free kicks awarded, the number of corners conceded or the number of throw-ins taken, then it becomes apparent that they play an important part in any match, and should be carefully rehearsed and intelligently put into operation. We have all seen magnificent goals scored from free kicks just outside the penalty area, from cleverly worked corners and from thoughtfully planned long throws and there is nothing more rewarding for a team to succeed with a set piece which it has been practising for hour after hour. We have also witnessed free kicks, corners and throw-ins being wasted in frustrating fashion when our side has perhaps held an overwhelming territorial advantage. It was significant that two of the three goals in the 1974 World Cup Final came directly from set pieces and equally interesting to note in that game between two well organized sides, the West Germans made good use of twelve of the sixteen free kicks they were awarded and the Dutch eight out of their ten. The West Germans had five shots at goal arising from their thirteen corners and the Dutch four shots from their nine. Impressively the West Germans did not waste a single throw-in during the whole match! Yet twenty-six free kicks, twenty-two corners and only twenty-one throw-ins in the entire game are unusually low and reflect the attitude of both teams to keep play moving. It has been said that in top class soccer something in the region of forty to fifty per cent of goals scored result from set plays and even in our own teams, how often have we seen the result settled by a single goal from a corner or a free kick? It is certainly worth looking in some detail at the various aspects of these dead ball situations.

Throw-ins

It astonishes me how little thought so many teams direct towards the throw-in. In most games the number of throws heavily outweigh corners and free kicks and yet how often do they seem to be rehearsed?

There are several basic principles regarding the throw in:

a) Always play safe by throwing forward rather than square near your own penalty area.

b) The nearest player available should take the throw quickly if possible, before the opposition can mark and re-group.

c) Players receiving the throw should not cramp the thrower, but aim to arrive as late as possible.

d) Thrower and receiver should work in harmony. Success against good marking is a matter of split second timing.

e) The throw should be made as easy as possible for the receiver to control.

The most common throw involves a return pass to the thrower himself, but this can be countered by defensive marking of the thrower. However, this should then leave our full back free for the return pass. We retain possession with this throw, though, of course, it is not very ambitious, and we have not achieved much penetration.

Late movement by players receiving the throw will often create the space and the confusion amongst marking defenders that we are searching for, and the simple interchange between our left striker o11 and left midfield player o10 in figure 54 can produce such opportunities.

Figure 54 Throw-in to o11. Intelligent criss-cross running by o10 and o11 will often create space

Once again the timing between the two runners and the thrower must be precise and the ball is usually best thrown crossfield for our left striker to take on his right foot into a dangerous position just outside the penalty area. Note that by such a manoeuvre we might quickly be able to switch the play across to the right wing, where space really does exist and where we can gain numerical superiority if our right back o2 is on the move and our right midfield player o8 is striking intelligently, as in figure 54. Remember too that we might be able to release our left midfield runner o10 to the goal line if the defensive marking is distracted by the criss-cross running of our forwards.

Perhaps the most crucial throw-in nowadays is the long throw. Almost every side seems to possess a long thrower and such a weapon can, naturally, prove a dangerous threat when anywhere near the opposing penalty area. Defences have had to counter this with tighter marking and cover in the danger area, and to some extent the potential of the long throw has been overcome. However, if your side is prepared to use this weapon intelligently and to produce *variations on the theme*, then goal scoring chances will still emerge from the long throw.

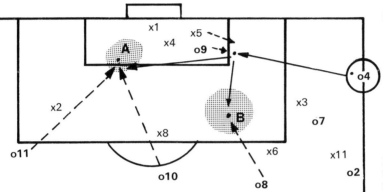

Figure 55 The long throw, orthodox tactics

Figure 55 shows the orthodox positions for a long throw and this can be quite successful if we employ some tactics. If our centre forward 09 is prepared to move forward late, yet fast, to meet the throw he can still steal a vital yard from marking defender X5 and either flick the ball on with his head into the shaded space A just in front of the goalkeeper for 010 or 011 to attack or, depending upon the type of ball he is receiving, he can nod the ball sideways and downwards into shaded area B giving 08 a snap shot at the goal.

Against anything but the sharpest defenders, these tactics for the long throw, if carefully rehearsed, will lead to goals. The more enterprising teams will add variations on this theme and here are some suggestions.

Firstly, and very simply, a *short* throw to 07 and a possible return pass will often enable us to reach the bye-line virtually unopposed, because so many defenders are marking the threat of our long throw (see figure 56). It is amazing how often such a short throw will cause confusion, merely because the opposing defence is entirely geared to the possibilities of the longer alternative. Our centre forward can then make a telling run either to find space himself or to take important defenders out of the danger area and leave gaps for powerful headers of the ball, such as our centre half 05, to meet 04's deep cross.

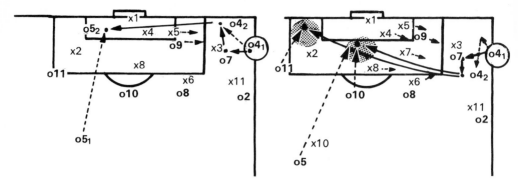

Figure 56 (left)
Variations on the long
throw using 07 and 05

Figure 57 (right)
Variations on the long
throw against a tight
marking defence

Secondly, figure 57 shows a similar long throw situation where team X are marking effectively and thus reducing the dangerous space in the penalty area we have utilized in the previous situations. Nonetheless, our team can re-open and exploit some of this space. 07 has had the ball thrown short to his feet, 04 has threatened to move behind defender X3 and then back-tracked quickly to receive a return pass from 07, played into space. While this is going on defenders in the penalty area will have been dragged automatically a few paces towards the ball, giving 04 the chance now with his left foot to switch the point of attack and chip the ball into any of the dangerous shaded areas from a new angle to which defenders will not be able to adjust immediately. The success of such a 'variation on the theme' hinges crucially on the attackers 05, 010 and 011 holding back their incisive runs until the last possible moment. Co-ordination between thrower and receiver and between 04 and his attacking runners is vital and will not occur without careful and meaningful practice. But successful teams must work hard at detailed practices such as this one.

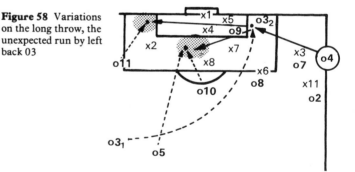

Figure 58 Variations
on the long throw, the
unexpected run by left
back 03

Thirdly, let us remember that the sudden appearance of a second target man on the goal-line can often create confusion in even the most organized of defences.

It might be our centre half, but in figure 58 it is our left back 03 who has arrived late to receive the long throw in front of our centre forward who is a decoy, and his tight markers. If the run and the throw are synchronized, then our left back should be able to flick on, head inside, or even turn with the ball before a marking defender picks him up. Once again 05, 010 and 011 must not arrive too early to close up the dangerous space available, and yet again the timing of such a set play needs detailed and patient practice.

Corners

The crowd always roars with anticipation when a corner is conceded and occasionally it enjoys the excitement of a player soaring high in the over-populated penalty area to head a magnificent goal. Yet how many in the crowd are aware of the meticulous planning that goes into corner kicks?

As with so many aspects of football, so with corners it is important to play to your strength. If you have a particularly gifted crosser of the ball, use him to take the corner, ideally a left-footed inswinger from the right side and a right-footed inswinger from the left. If you possess a goalkeeper who is not strong in the air, then it is all the more essential to use your tall striking forwards in defensive tactics at corners and long throws. However, I am always amazed by the strangely short sighted tactics of so many coaches who pull the *whole* side back to pack the penalty area when the opposition has a corner. Not only do they run the risk of getting in each other's way, but often we see forwards back in their own defence conceding a goal *because* they are not quite sharp enough in their tackling, not quite tight enough in their marking or quite ruthless enough in their heading challenges. In addition, withdrawing every player enables opponents to push more men forward *and*, equally important, reduces the chances of the quick counter attack. It must make more sense for two small, fast attacking players to link upfield rather than cluttering our own penalty area.

However, it is as an attacking weapon that the corner needs to be analyzed tactically. As with throw-ins, there are a number of fundamental principles:

a) The corner must be floated away from the goalkeeper, whether inswinging or outswinging.

b) The target men moving in must start their runs from deep to ensure speed and lift when they meet the ball.

c) Near-post runs or short corner plays should be made as

late as possible and co-ordination between kicker and receiver is all-important.

d) Do not forget the value of the quickly taken corner, before the defenders are fully organized.

The corner that we see most is the simple chip for attackers to try to head into goal, and figure 59 reminds us of the need for two or three of our attackers to stagger themselves in order to run and meet the cross as it enters the shaded danger area just beyond the goalkeeper's reach. If the run and the kick are timed correctly the attackers are bound to be better placed to head accurately than defenders who are having to keep half an eye on the ball and the other half on the movements of the forward they are marking. Whymark, Mariner and Beattie have scored decisive goals in this manner.

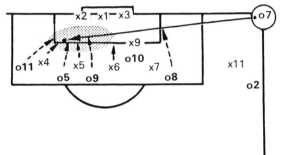

Figure 59 The orthodox corner. Note the value of the far post chip into the shaded space, which 09, 05 or 011 can exploit; but 08's near-post run for the driven cross, is an important alternative

Intelligent variation is as much a part of the successful corner as it is of the successful throw-in, and the hard, low driven corner for the attacking forward 08 to meet with head or foot at the near post is a useful alternative to the straightforward chip. Yet, if the opposing defence is dominating the area, and the goalkeeper is strong in the air, or if yours is a small-attacking side, then the short corner as an alternative can often help to draw defenders out from the danger zone and produce the subtle variation which I have already referred to earlier.

There are several types of short corner, and we must always be aware of the use of our full back in this ploy, (see figure 60).

If our striking attackers wait for the precise moment before making their runs then the full back 02's cross might catch the defenders slightly off guard, as they will have taken up positions to cover the corner cross and will not have readjusted to the new angle, that is, if the chip comes over early. Yet the most orthodox and most exploited short corner involves the use of the support player on the goal-line. There are several variations within

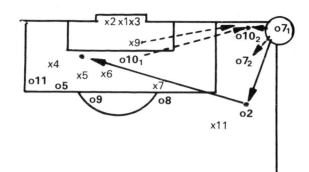

Figure 60 The short
corner using full back
02, or forward 010

the theme here, but I like the ball played to 010's feet. If
he has arrived late and unmarked he can then turn and attack
the defender on the goal-line, using 07 as a decoy in order to
dribble past the opponent and then look for the short driven cross
or the dangerous pull back for an incoming colleague. Alternatively
he can pass the ball to 07 who has moved out into a support
position himself. Unless there are two marking defenders available,
and often there are not if the kick is taken quickly, this short
corner *again carefully rehearsed* can pose real problems to any
defence on the ground or in the air.

**The headed goal
from a corner** – in
this case by Don
Masson (left) of
Scotland against
England at Hampden
Park; it is significant
that the taller Jordan
is being marked by 2
English defenders,
while the unmarked
Masson seemingly has
time to place his
header.

Free kicks

Unfortunately free kicks play a very large part in the game of
football, though happily they do not dictate the final scoreline
in quite the way that our Rugby cousins so often have to accept.
Nonetheless, the more important the match, the more the tension
and, whether we like it or not, the more likelihood of a series
of free kicks being awarded, frequently near the edge of the penalty

box. Naturally we should aim to make good use of all our free kicks, but it is obviously those near the danger zone which need particular care and attention, from the defensive and the attacking points of view.

Defending at free kicks

There are three main priorities when defending against free kicks and for that matter against corners or throw-ins:

a) Concentration It is quite remarkable how even the most gifted and experienced of players often 'switch off' momentarily and sometimes disastrously during a stoppage in play, and this is specially true towards the end of any game, when the mind as well as the muscles tend to tire. I suspect that this quality of concentration is an often neglected one in any consideration of the complete player.

b) An intelligently organized 'wall' Some teams will use their goalkeeper to line up the defensive wall with the assistance of the player on the end of the line, but this always leaves open the possibility of his not being positioned correctly for the free kick taken quickly and it is probably better if the wall is organized by an outfield player. Certainly the keeper must make the initial decision of whether to demand a wall or not. This will normally hinge upon whether the infringement has taken place in the defensive third of the field or not, but the strength of the wind, the presence of a renowned powerful shot on the opposing side, the firmness of the ground, are all factors which have to be taken into account. Yet, once the keeper calls for a wall, his defence should know exactly how many players go into it and in what order. Nowadays it is crucial to guard against the 'bent' free kick, but it is still a mistake to mass too many defenders into a defensive wall, as they will only serve to blur the goalkeeper's view and reduce the number of players available for marking elsewhere.

Figure 61 gives an idea of the numbers required in defensive walls for free kicks from differing angles and also shows the wall

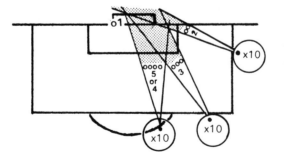

Figure 61 The defensive wall, well organized for X10's free kicks, leaving goalkeeper 01 with clear vision of the ball at the far-post, yet covering the near-post securely

correctly sited. Whereas the dangerous space is sealed off in figure 61 and any 'bent' free kick is covered, in figure 62 the poor goalkeeper cannot be sure which side of his goal to cover. Thus it is important for the player 'lining up' the wall to ensure that his anchor man is covering the near-post and is standing just wide enough to cover the possibility of a 'bent' kick. Equally it is important to realize that a well-organized wall requires no cheating, kicking the ball away or stealing of extra yards!

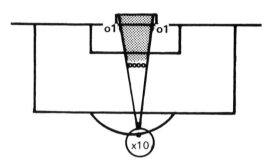

Figure 62 The defensive wall, wrongly organized, leaving the goalkeeper with problems

c) Marking players It is essential to remember that a successful wall is only part of the answer to defensive success at free kicks, and that tight marking is equally vital. Obviously, if the free kick is at an angle it helps to have your bigger, central defenders out of the wall in order to mark and challenge in the air and it is best to put midfield players and attackers in the wall (but they must take up their positions quickly) so that defenders are free to mark closely. Any infringement against us near the edge of the penalty area is going to require all our players to think defensively, and that means being prepared to pull players back, to watch late runs from opposing defenders, to cover any short free kick and to watch for any other unexpected move by the opposition.

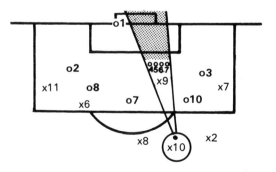

Figure 63 The defensive wall and a well organized marking system

Figure 63 shows a tight marking system, with space denied to the opposition, but note the importance of our two players 07 and 010, preferably our best ball winners, ready to attack the ball once it has been played and to pressurize the intended shot as quickly as possible and the need for 02 and 03 in the diagram to stay level with the wall, thus threatening over-eager forwards with offside.

So much for the fundamental issues involved in defensive play against free kicks just outside the penalty area. Inside the area we can do nothing very much to defend against the penalty kick, apart from the intelligent anticipation of any rebound, but we should always be aware of the best defence against the indirect free kick in the penalty area, usually awarded for obstruction, unfair calling, or too many steps by the goalkeeper. It is important to have all players goal-side of the ball, in a solid wall of eleven, if the kick is inside the six yard area, or of ten with one quick and combative player left free to attack the ball once it has been played, if the kick is further away from the goal but still in the penalty area. The crucial thing is that the players move as one towards the ball as soon as it is in play.

Having ensured that no free kick is likely to succeed against our defence, let us now look at ways of making intelligent use of decisions in our favour on the edge of our opponents' penalty area.

The Wall – Bruce Rioch, then of Derby County scored with this free kick against Newcastle United, but notice the confusion caused by Number 9, Hector, and the gaps that have appeared in the defensive wall.

Attacking free kicks

All teams and coaches have their own favourite attacking ploys from free kicks, and we have seen some highly successful ones on 'Match of the Day' such as Willie Carr of Coventry back flipping the ball into the air for Ernie Hunt to volley home in spectacular fashion, or Peter Osgood lifting the ball marginally from the ground for Jim McCalliog to volley a match winning goal during Southampton's successful 1976 Cup run. But, let us be realistic and *not attempt too many* different kicks. I think that it is important to keep your free kicks as simple as possible, for there is nothing more damaging to team morale than to see a scoring situation disappear through over elaboration. The fewer moves made before the kick is taken, the better! Yet before any free kick is likely to succeed the following factors have to be borne in mind:

a) Players not directly involved in the intended ploy, should always try to *stretch* the defence and look as if they are going to receive the ball. Decoys and dummies, if cleverly contrived, are most helpful.

b) The player who is going to play the crucial part should appear on the scene as late and as inconspicuously as possible.

c) Whatever systems have been discussed, if the opposing wall is weak and there is clearly a chance of a direct shot on goal — then let fly!

d) Play to your strengths, and organize your free kicks according to the qualities of the players in your team.

I shall concentrate on the basic free kicks, although there are, of course, many variations that can be developed from these:

1 We must always start by looking for the chance of a direct shot, as I have said above, and this is usually assisted by a dummy run over the ball by one, or two players before our specialist picks his spot. If you have left and right footed 'benders' in the team you can clearly use both and, according to the situation, leave them to decide which is going to dummy and which to shoot.

2 You will certainly need one fairly straightforward kick which involves two players with one touching the ball for the second to shoot. In such a case the important thing is to ensure that your most powerful and accurate shot receives the ball on his strongest foot and, if possible, clear of the worst of the defensive wall. I prefer the option of two men looking for a short square pass. One such as 08 in figure 64, three or four yards to the left of the ball and the other 02 moving at the last moment into a similar space to the right. The player delegated to take the kick turns to tap the ball to his expectant colleague 08 but instead backheels it for the lurking 02 in our diagram to take a shot on goal. Simple, yet with practice most effective, particularly if your team possesses some convincing actors!

87

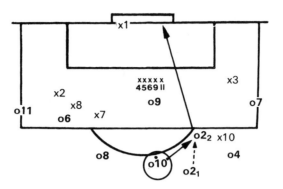

Figure 64 Attacking free kick, simple and effective

3 A popular innovation in recent years, introduced I believe by the Brazilians in the 1974 World Cup, has been the stationing of one or two attackers at the end of the defensive wall, thus unsighting the goalkeeper and creating uncertainty in the defence. As the shot comes in from either of the free kicks we have considered above, these 'extensions to the wall' duck or break away at the very last moment giving the goalkeeper precious little time to adjust to the shot, especially if it is swerving as well.

4 It is often advantageous for the attacking team to post a small and quick player *in front of* the defensive wall, prepared to come to meet a short free kick and either turn it sideways for an incoming colleague to shoot, or better still to lay the ball ·off at an angle for a late running player, 04 in the diagram, to take a shot at the goal. Even if this player in front of the wall is not used directly he will certainly act as another important part of any decoy operation.

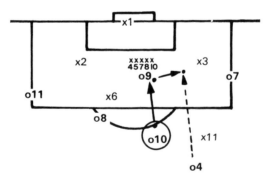

Figure 65 Attacking free kick. A player, 09 in this case, can be very useful in front of the defensive wall

5 But for those who enjoy the complex set piece, and I would certainly always recommend one involved ploy, which players of every age and level enjoy practising, how about the following?

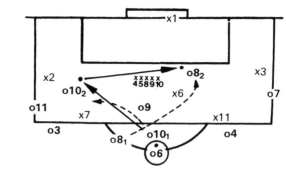

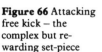

Figure 66 Attacking free kick – the complex but rewarding set-piece

010 dummies over the ball and runs left, 08 dummies over the ball and runs right, 06 looks to shoot hard but instead plays the ball to 010 in his new and probably unguarded position, who then side-foots a pass *behind* the defensive wall for 08, who has made a semi-circular run around the wall and thus has again probably arrived in space unmarked to hammer the ball into the net! Rewarding? Certainly, and as with all free kicks distinctly workable *if* rehearsed conscientiously.

Finally when discussing attacking free kicks, we should not forget that such infringements frequently occur on the angle of the penalty box, or even wider when the wall, as we have seen, will often comprise only two or three defensive players. For an attacking free kick on the corner of the penalty area the defensive marking is likely to look similar to that in figure 67 and as we can see there is not much space to be found. However, an effective tactic for uncovering a few precious yards of space in the danger area can be implemented as follows:

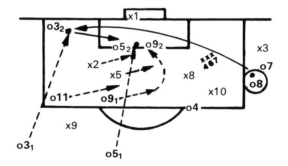

Figure 67 Attacking free kick, showing the value of decoy runs and intelligent planning

6 After using some of the decoys we have already discussed, ensure that your strongest aerial player is ready to make a late run from a central position as 05 in figure 67, and that 011 and

09 creep in bringing their marking defenders with them, and giving space for your left back 03 to make a late, wide run, meeting the long floated free kick and heading it back across the box where 05 and 09 should find a defence still re-adjusting to the sudden switch of play, and thus have the prospect of a strike on goal.

While never pretending that I have covered all the aspects of free kicks, corners and the throw-ins, I have devoted a lot of time in this chapter to the details of set pieces in attack and in defence and any coach who is interested in a successful team must be prepared to spend an equally large proportion of his time on these important aspects of the game. It is worth repeating in conclusion that forty to fifty per cent of all goals are scored as a result of these set pieces—statistics that speak for themselves.

7 The coach and his team

One aspect of a successful football team which often tends to be neglected amongst all the tactics, skills and systems is the composition of any eleven players in terms of character and personality. If you look at any winning team you will discover that the players fit into a jig-saw pattern, the calming influence of one, the competitive aggression of the next, the confident arrogance of another and the unselfish determination of a fourth. An integrated team has to work together happily off the field as well as on and the various qualities of team spirit are often assisted by a humorist in any side, or a lively extrovert to counterbalance the quiet, thoughtful player. Then again in your ideal team you need several competitive, explosive players, as long as you have a calming influence in the team to curb their excesses, such as Bremner or Ball. Team spirit is a subtle thing, primarily engendered by the coach himself, but reliant on the personality balance amongst the players. Often a gifted player is dropped or placed on the transfer list simply because of his failure to fit into this pattern, and often a side give twenty per cent extra when one selfish or disruptive individual is left out. Clearly no side can succeed with too many players or personalities of the same type. It would be as wrong to have three comedians in the changing room as it would be to have three ball playing individualists in the forward line, and it would be suicidal to play eleven or even five footballers of fiery temperament in the same team. Equally, just as any convincing attack needs at least one aggressive live-wire, so any successful defence needs the quiet reader of situations as well as the forceful talker. It is this sort of personality balance that is vital for twin centre halves, and time and again in a successful side, we see the calming influence of a Bobby Moore or a Colin Todd integrating with the aggression of a Jack Charlton, or a Roy Macfarland. Nor is it just coincidence that the coach of the very successful West German team, Helmut Schoen, lays great emphasis on this balance.

Indeed, we often forget when watching 'Match of the Day' or any big football match, how much talking does take place during the game. You have only to watch professionals playing a practice game to realize the non-stop chat. Every coach will agree that forceful and helpful calling on the pitch is an essential ingredient of a good side. In this respect the role of the captain is more important than is often realized. True, some teams hardly seem to need a captain, either because there are several influential players in key positions or because the coach is leaping up and down on the touchline and virtually captaining his side from there! Yet in the heat of the moment, when the referee's decisions seem to be harsh or when the opposition bring on a tactical substitute, a respected captain, who can calm his side and knows his coach's tactics well enough to have a quiet word with the appropriate colleague, is worth a tremendous amount. Look at the influence of Franz Beckenbauer in the West German National team or Bobby Moore in Ramsey's successful England team.

The appointment of captain can be of considerable importance; the appointment of the coach is absolutely crucial. In the final reckoning the team spirit, personality balance and the *motivation* of any side stems from the coach. This is not the place to analyze the successful managers, but one thing shines through clearly, that whether we are talking of Alf Ramsey, Bill Shankley, Don Revie, Jock Stein, Bobby Robson, Tommy Docherty or Brian Clough we find that they have one thing in common — man management. No side is going to give of its best unless the coach has motivated the players, and this will only happen if the atmosphere at the club during tactical talks, training and in the changing room, is right. Every manager or coach has his own characteristic way of running things, no two men are alike. But any winning team must possess a coach who is prepared to work as hard as his players, whether it be practising with them or putting the interest of his side or club before everything else.

The coach will be more respected by his players if he is tough but honest, and the coach who says one thing to his team and another behind their backs or to the press is never going to gain that respect. There is no need for iron discipline in football, but fitness is absolutely essential to any ambitious team and a coach must ensure that his players train hard and then preserve that fitness in the way in which they go about their private lives. There is never going to be any place in a motivated side for the selfish player who drinks, smokes and dances late on a Friday night! Disciplined tactics on the field are also important and although a good coach will usually discuss tactics with the rest of his team before a game, he is the one who must finally take the decisions, lay down the strategy and ensure that his players are fully aware of how to react in a given situation.

Team spirit cannot be acquired by waving a magic wand, but will develop if the coach is prepared to treat his players like men and not like robots, and to remember that each one probably needs slightly different handling. Frequently, footballers who are the most difficult to handle off the field give the coach most when they are involved in the game itself. Team spirit will grow if the coach is on close terms with his captain, and as the players representative, it is most important that the captain should be able to speak openly and honestly to the coach about the complaints, worries and tensions which must at times beset any ambitious football team. Mutual respect between captain and coach will certainly help to create the right atmosphere in a club.

Team spirit will grow if the coach is on close terms with his captain – and here Don Revie watches Gerry Francis with interest in an England practice session.

A coach will obviously earn the respect of his players if he is able to pinpoint errors when things are going wrong, and if he is prepared to boost the confidence of one of his team who is going through a bad patch, by a quiet word before the game or at half-time. Yet it is no good pretending to be popular with your team the whole time, just as it is fatal to make decisions primarily to protect your own reputation. A good coach must be prepared to tell his players fairly and squarely when they are going to be dropped from the side and why, and he must also have the courage to discipline any player who constantly abuses the referee. Sadly there are too many managers and coaches, even amongst the most successful, who are too prepared to back their own players and thus undermine the referee in such circumstances.

Finally, a successful side must be given confidence by the coach, confidence in themselves and in his tactics. In this respect pre-match preparations are important for it is at this stage that any worthwhile coach must ensure that his players are in the right frame of mind, not too tense, but not too relaxed, fiercely determined to win and disciplined in their awareness of the tactics to be imple-

93

mented, but not so over-coached that they cannot express their own individualism imaginatively and unexpectedly.

To summarize, a successful coach must be able to bring forth the best from his players with a subtle combination of common-sense and 'psychology'. He must be able to put himself into his players' shoes so that he can understand their feelings and their problems. There is no need for him to have been an outstanding player as long as he is honest, sincere and has a perceptive knowledge of the game. Once there is real trust and respect between a coach and his team, and once the personality balance is correct then success is never far away.

Conclusion

Inevitably, I have not been able to discuss every aspect of a football team and some readers might be disappointed to find, for instance, little coverage of fitness training, only a passing reference to goal-keeping and no comprehensive list of basic practices. However, these have been fully analyzed in various other excellent books on soccer and, as I suggested in my introduction, I have primarily attempted to explain the importance of positive yet flexible tactics and to emphasize the way in which these tactics can be intelligently and successfully implemented.

Fortunately there is never a complete answer to any footballing question and it one of the joys of this great game that different teams can produce exciting, winning performances with very dis-similar tactics. I would never presume to suggest that this book contains all, or even most of the answers, but I hope that, whether you are a player, coach, or an enthusiastic supporter, I will have helped you to think and talk about the game more perceptively, to play it more imaginatively, to watch it more intelligently and thus to appreciate it more fully. Those of us who have played, coached and watched soccer have gained enormous pleasure and made numerous lasting friendships. Yet whether we win or lose, the more we know about the game the greater its rewards, and if this book helps you to enjoy your soccer more then it has been well worthwhile.